The Unfinished Revolution: The Civil Rights Movement From 1955 to 1965

Peter Ralph Bartling

iUniverse, Inc.
New York   Bloomington

iUniverse books may be ordered through booksellers or by contacting:

iUniverse
1663 Liberty Drive
Bloomington, IN 47403
www.iuniverse.com
1-800-Authors (1-800-288-4677)

ISBN: 978-1-4401-7763-7 (sc)
ISBN: 978-1-4401-7777-4 (dj)
ISBN: 978-1-4401-7764-4 (ebook)

Printed in the United States of America

iUniverse rev. date: 01/12/10

THE UNFINISHED REVOLUTION:
THE CIVIL RIGHTS MOVEMENT

FROM 1955 TO 1965

by

Peter Ralph Bartling

————————————

Table of Contents

LIST OF FIGURES

LIST OF ILLUSTRATIONS

CHAPTER 1

Introduction

Objectives of the Study

Systematic organization of the African American revolution began in America approximately ten years ago. The years since have brought about many changes desired by the movement; yet, today the African American still faces discrimination, prejudice, and bigotry. As a result, his protest has never been more vigorous than it is at the present time.

The African American revolution is not history; it is "not distant enough to be bathed in a glowing forgetfulness of things past." [1] It is in existence now; consequently, it is necessary that political scientists have an understanding of the most crucial domestic issue confronting our society.

The general hypothesis around which this thesis is structured is that:

Revolution does not produce change; rather, change produces revolution.

Change is a traumatic process because most people do not understand it, and therefore they are afraid of it. It produces perplexing problems and vexations that make a population susceptible to the appeal of a revolution.

The methods employed by the African American revolution have changed considerably with the passage of time. Initially, litigation was used. Then the scene shifted from the courtroom to the street, where nonviolent direct action was implemented in various forms. The next stage for the battle for civil rights was, and is, in the minority community itself. The movement is trying to build a grass roots organization in the ghetto areas that will enable African Americans (and any other deprived groups) to help themselves economically by using political power. At the same time that the bulk of the African American organizations are shifting their orientation toward the "audacious

---

1   "Marx's Revenge," *Time*, LXXXV (May 21, 1965), 69.

use of political power," a segment of the movement is advocating armed self-defense because of the lack of justice for the African American in the South.

The objectives of this thesis, then, will be to show how change brings revolution, and what form that revolution may take.

Definition of Terms

A number of terms occur throughout this thesis that should be defined. The term *revolution*, as it appears in the title,

> . . . does not connote violence; it refers to the qualitative transformation as fundamental institutions, more or less rapidly, to the point where the social and economic structure which they comprised can no longer be said to be the same.[2]

The term *civil rights movement* means "the movement on behalf of meaningful equality for the American Negro both in the North and in the South."[3]

Race relations refer to "the problems that arise from the contacts of people who differ from each other either racially or culturally."[4] *Segregation* is a type of isolation that denotes being set apart. It can be either voluntary or involuntary. It can be either spatial or physical separation, or social segregation where values and traditions isolate groups from each other.

The term *American Creed* refers to the "national conscience." It should be interpreted broadly because it is an expanding dogma and not a permanent and precise creed. However:

> . . . the creed is clear and explicit in practically all respects for the Negro problem. Most of the value premises with which we shall be concerned have actually been incorporated for a long time in the national Constitution and in the constitutions and laws of the states. [5]

---

2   Bayard Rustin, *From Protest to Politics: The Future of the Civil Rights Movement, Commentary*, XXXIX (February, 1965), 28.

3   Willmoore Kendall, *The Civil Rights Movement and the Coming Constitutional Crisis, The Intercollegiate Review*, I (February-March, 1965), 54.

4   Brewton Berry, *Race and Ethnic Relations* (Boston: Houghton, Mifflin Company, 1958), pp. 5-6.

5   Arnold Rose, *The African American in America: The Condensed version of Gunnar Myrdal's An American Dilemma* (New York: Harper and Row, 1964), pp. 8-9.

Reference to *eleven states of the Old Confederacy* includes Alabama, Arkansas, Florida, Georgia, Louisiana, Mississippi, North Carolina, South Carolina, Tennessee, Texas, and Virginia. The term *Deep South* refers to the states of Louisiana, Mississippi, Alabama, Georgia, and South Carolina.

Civil rights refer to any rights or privileges guaranteed by the Constitution or by the laws of the United States.

Organization, Scope and Limitations of the Study

The approach to be used in analyzing the "unfinished revolution" is topical. Chapter II is an attempt to explain the characteristics common to all social movements and the psychological pattern common to their adherents. Chapter III attempts to go beyond the headlines and bylines of newspaper and journal articles and to dissect a living organization that is actually responsible for this news.

Chapter IV concerns itself with the changing character of the civil rights movement. It will discuss the types of civil rights organizations and their rapid growth, and will conclude by exposing the internal cleavages present between the moderates and the militants and relating these to the future of the movement. The final chapter will present a brief summary of the findings of the research involved in this thesis.

The study is limited to an analysis of the civil rights movement as it operated in America from 1955 to 1965. This period was chosen because the birth of the movement can be dated back to December, 1955. Consequently, events up to that time, while important in the African American's struggle for freedom, were only indirectly responsible for what was to become a full-scale social movement.

By affiliating with a civil rights organization in Los Angeles, the observer was able to gather data on the internal workings of one group within the movement. Case studies on other civil rights groups in Los Angeles were not within the scope of this study. The local chapter of the Congress of Racial Equality (CORE) will be the only group focused on, in a case study capacity, in an attempt to understand the mechanics of an African American protest organization.

Source Material

A number of works served as the underlying foundation upon which this study was developed. An article by Gordon W. Allport[6] provided an authoritative

---

6   Gordon W. Allport (special editor), *Controlling Group Prejudice, The Annals of*

and illuminating discussion of race relations as they existed in America in 1946. Arnold Rose,[7] in *The Negro Protest*, presented material on the historical context of the African American movement, on problems that the African American has in specific areas of American life, and on the different organizations working to secure equality for all African Americans.

The Negro Revolution in America[8] is based on a nationwide survey conducted by *Newsweek* magazine. It presents valuable findings on what it is like to be an African American, the weapons of the revolution, and who the real leaders of the movement are. Louis Lomax[9] examined in detail the civil rights movement and presented information on the events, organizations, and leaders that have molded the African American's fight for equality. Rose,[10] in an updated version of Gunnar Myrdal's work originally published in 1944, touched on nearly every aspect of the African American's life in America. *Portrait of a Decade: The Second American Revolution*[11] traces the civil rights movement as it progressed from 1954 to 1964, and discusses such subjects as the school desegregation cases, the role of the federal government as it relates to civil rights, and the right to vote.

While several books and articles provided material on social movements for Chapter II, six works were especially important. Herbert Blumer[12] has constructed a very informative section on "Collective Behavior" in *New Outline of the Principles of Sociology*. *The Psychology of Social Movements*[13] is divided into two sections: the first describes individual motivation and action,

---

the *American Academy of Political and Social Science*, CCXLIV (March, 1946), 1-182.

7   Arnold M. Rose (special editor), *The African American Protest, The Annals of the American Academy of Political and Social Science*, CCCLVII (January, 1965), 1-126.

8   William Brink and Louis Harris, *The African American Revolution in America* (New York: Simon and Schuster, 1964).

9   Louis E. Lomax, *The African American Revolt* (New York: The New American Library of World Literature, Incorporated, 1963).

10   Rose, op. cit., pp. 1-321

11   Anthony Lewis and *The New York Times, Portrait of a Decade: The Second American Revolution* (New York: Random House, 1964).

12   Herbert Blumer, *Collective Behavior*, in *New Outline of the Principles of Sociology*, edited by Alfred McClung Lee (New York: Barnes and Noble, 1951), pp. 167-222.

13   Hadley Cantril, *The Psychology of Social Movements* (New York: John Wiley and Son, Incorporated, 1941).

while the second discusses a number of former social movements. Arnold W. Green[14] has presented a good analysis of social movements in *Sociology, An Analysis of Life in Modern Society.* Eric Hoffer's classic,[15] *The True Believer,* studies the psychology behind mass movements and analyzes some of the peculiarities associated with every mass movement. *Social Movements in the United States*[16] studies movements in the broad context of social change. It uses the Grange, Christian Science, and the Ku Klux Klan to illustrate the several concepts and generalizations the author wished to explain. The final study to be mentioned here is *Social Movements,*[17] which offers a broad sociological theory of political and social movements.

Most of the data contained in Chapter III came from the writer's research as a participant observer in CORE. However, a few articles, pamphlets, and books were very useful.

An article by Marvin Rich[18] and one by Martin Mayer[19] present good analyses of organization. Both articles discuss such factors as history, growth, strategy, and future orientation. A number of pamphlets[20] put out by the national and Los Angeles chapters of CORE provided useful information. Three additional works proved invaluable as sources for information on nonviolent direct action. *War Without Violence*[21] and *Non- Violence in Peace and War*[22] deal primarily with the philosophy of passive resistance. On

---

14   Arnold W. Green, *Sociology, An Analysis of Life in Modern Society* (New York: McGraw-Hill Book Company, Incorporated, 1960).

15   Eric Hoffer, *The True Believer* (New York: The New American Library of World Literature, Incorporated, 1963).

16   C. Wendell King, *Social Movements in the United States* (New York: Random House, 1964).

17   Rudolf Heberle, *Social Movements in the United States* (New York: Random House, 1964).

18   Marvin Rich, *The Congress of Racial Equality and Its Strategy, The Annals of the American Academy of Political and Social Science,* CCCLVII (January, 1965), 113-118.

19   Martin Mayer, "CORE: The Shock Troops of the African American Revolt," *Post,* November 21, 1964, pp. 79-83.

20   CORE, *CORE Rules for Action* (New York: National CORE, 1963); CORE, *This Is CORE* (New York: National CORE, n.d.); CORE, *All About CORE* (New York: National CORE, n.d.).

21   Krishnalal Shridharanai, *War Without Violence* (New York: Harcourt, Brace and Company, 1939).

22   M. K. Gandhi, *Non-Violence in Peace and War* (Volume II, Ahmedabad:

the other hand, *A Manual for Direct Action*[23] is concerned with the actual implementation of non-violent direct action by protest movements.

The greater part of the information presented in Chapter IV concerns itself with African American protest organizations. Many of the major sources dealing with these groups have already been cited. In addition, *Fight for Freedom*[24] is a chronological record of the birth and growth of the NAACP; and much of the material on the SCLC came from *The SCLC Story.*[25] *SNCC: The New Abolitionists*[26] supplied data on the history, programs, and goals of the Student Nonviolent Coordinating Committee. *The Black Muslims in America*[27] is a comprehensive study of the Black Muslims as an organization, and as a group within the larger context of the whole civil rights movement.

Before terminating this section, one other very valuable source should be mentioned. The *Los Angeles Times* opened a news bureau in Atlanta, Georgia, in 1965 to provide firsthand coverage of the civil rights movement in the South. Articles written by Pulitzer Prize winner Jack Nelson, news bureau director, have covered in depth almost every phase of the African American protest. In addition, Nelson's background and training have enabled him to interpret and accurately evaluate many of the latest trends in the African American's struggle for equality.

Methodology

In the "Editor's Foreword" to *The Study of Comparative Government*, Richard C. Snyder stated "that political science is passing through a period of change and reappraisal."[28] Attempting not only to make an original contribution to the discipline instead of just a synthesis of existing data but also to be in the vanguard of the latest trends in political science, the writer has employed a method of gathering material known as participant observation. Participant observation refers to:

Navajivan Publishing House, 1949).

23   Martin Oppenheimer and George Lakey, *A Manual for Direct Action* (Chicago: Quadrangel Books, Incorporated, 1964).

24   Langston Hughes, *Fight for Freedom* (New York: Berkley Publishing Corporation, 1962).

25   Ed Clayton (editor), *The SCLC Story* (Atlanta: SCLC, 1964).

26   Howard Zinn, *SNCC: The New Abolitionists* (Boston: Beacon Press, 1964).

27   C. Eric Lincoln, *The Black Muslims in America* (Boston: Beacon Press, 1963).

28   Roy C. Macridis, *The Study of Comparative Government* (PS 21 of *Studies in Political Science*; New York: Random House, 1964), p.v.

...that method in which the observer participates in the daily life of the people under study, either openly in the role of researcher or covertly in some disguised role, observing things that happen, listening to what is said, and questioning people over some length of time.[29]

The writer's role as a researcher was known to the people in the organization under study. The results of seven months of empirical field investigation are incorporated in Chapter III.

A number of problems were encountered as a participant observer while a member of CORE. The most obvious one was skin color. Being Caucasian made it necessary to spend a great deal of time building up confidence before interviewing and questioning African Americans with the assurance of obtaining valid information. Secondly, fear had to be overcome. Coming out of a CORE meeting late at night in the ghetto and walking to one's car did not give the most solid feeling of security. The bitter resentment of African Americans toward the whites was a new experience, and such labels as "Crackers" and "Klanner," and such statements as "Look, there goes a white man, there goes a white man" took a great deal of getting used to. One might even call it "cultural shock."

There were several matters interviewees were unable, or unwilling, to talk about. For example, when asked about the exact number of members in the organization, the office manager replied: "I can only give you an estimate." This statement was given even though he is the one who mails out the monthly calendar to every member. Many members, while glad to talk in generalities, never would get specific or allow themselves to be quoted verbatim.

In the writer's opinion, however, the advantages of participant observation far outweigh the liabilities of such a technique because one can see what is, rather than what is purported to be. Moreover, one can observe actual changes in orientation, function, and behavior over time which allow at least fairly accurate predictions about future trends and events. This is invaluable, because political scientists are always concerned with problems of process. Often the trouble with working in an institution is that one becomes institutionalized and fails to recognize what is really there. Participant observation overcomes this difficulty. Although the problem under investigation determines the method of investigation, political scientists could more adequately perform their research role if greater use were made of this tool.

29   Howard S. Becker and Blanche Geer, *Participant Observation and Interviewing: A Comparison, Human Organization*, XVI (Fall, 1957), 28.

Significance of the Study

This particular piece of research is significant because it demonstrates the relationship between the political system and a social movement.

When President Abraham Lincoln issued the Emancipation Proclamation on January 1, 1863, slavery was officially abolished and all slaves were declared free. Yet, ninety-two years later the African American still was not free. Nevertheless, as the decades passed, he became exposed to the American Creed. Consequently, a social movement eventually began to emerge that served as a vehicle by which he could channelize years of latent frustration and bitterness into productive activity on his own behalf. Herein lies the relevance for political science.

A viable political system must recognize and cope with opposition within the framework of the system. If it is not responsive to the demands of an influential group in society, there is the possibility that the group will become extralegal and work outside of the legitimate channels to power. The group does not wish to further the existing policies of the system. As a result, it is unlikely that it will abide by the traditional "rules of the game" (constitutions, laws, customs, and traditions) because the judicial and legislative institutions have offered the group no redress. When, and if, this occurs, the political system itself is jeopardized. Political scientists must have an understanding of social movements, why they arise, their potential strength, and the tools they employ to realize desired objectives. Equipped with this knowledge, they can educate society and furnish intelligent alternatives to decision makers on how best to handle potentially revolutionary situations so that the political system can be preserved.

A subsidiary reason for justifying this research lies on the grounds of its relevancy to contemporary research activities in the field of political science. The behavioral approach to politics is very much in vogue today. The case study on the Los Angeles chapter of CORE emphasized this trend by analyzing personal and group behavior in an organizational context. Moreover, in keeping with the behavioral tradition, this thesis was interdisciplinary because it relied on many concepts and research works from the field of sociology. It is hoped that this behavioral orientation in Chapter III will encourage and stimulate some thinking in new directions.

CHAPTER II

Social Movements

What sort of a day was December 1, 1955? It was a day like all days, filled with those events that alter and light up our times. Mrs. Rosa Parks, an African American seamstress in her early fifties, boarded the Cleveland Avenue bus in Montgomery, Alabama, just as she had done on numerous occasions. As the vehicle was segregated, she sat in the first black seat behind the white section.

The bus filled rapidly, leaving many white and African American patrons standing in the aisle near their appropriate sections. Then the bus driver issued his ultimatum: Mrs. Rosa Parks and three other African Americans were to relinquish their seats and permit the white standees to have them. Although the other three African Americans complied with the command, Rosa Parks sat fast.

Mrs. Parks subsequently was arrested for this violation against the contemporary mores and customs of Southern society and was quickly taken into custody by the local police. In five minutes the complete melodrama was over. However, Mrs. Parks' voice was heard "round the world," because "from this small incident the Negro revolt sprang full blown."[1]

Was the Rosa Parks incident atypical of the reaction of most present-day African Americans, or was it part of the deepening mood of despair and disillusionment that gripped the African American community after World War II? What exactly do these people want? Are they organized in such a way as to realize effectively their goals? Have they a program and objectives? What is it that they find repulsive in their present milieu? What constitutes a *Great Society* in their minds? Moreover,

> ...we may also want to know what immediate steps they intend to take
> in order to achieve their goal. Do they believe in gradual reform or in

---

1   Louis E. Lomax, *The African American Revolt* (New York: The New American Library of World Literature, Incorporated, 1963), p. 17.

a sudden and violent revolution? Do they believe that the time for achievement of their goal will come soon or do they reckon on a long period of preparation?[2]

The purpose of this chapter will be to structure an analytical frame of reference that can readily be utilized in studying any concrete social movement as it commences in the political system. The aim will be to develop a prototype concept. Such a conceptual tool should aid in answering pertinent questions about the kinds of social movements that are presently being observed.

Systematic theoretical study in the assessment of social movements is lacking; nevertheless, there are a multitude of definitions as to what constitutes a social movement. Herbert Blumer has defined social movements as "collective enterprises to establish a new order of life."[3] Rudolf Heberle felt that a social movement is a "collective ready for action by which some kind of change is to be achieved, some innovation to be made, or some previous condition to be restored."[4] These two definitions dwell upon the change-producing and group aspects of social movements. On the other hand, C. Wendell King, while being cognizant of the above two components, also emphasized organization and scope in his definition of a social movement: "a group venture extending beyond a local community or a single event and involving a systematic effort to inaugurate changes in thought, behavior, and social relationships."[5]

As a social movement of paramount magnitude, the African American revolt has special significance for the American political system. In the African American culture pattern an inertia of the masses is omnipresent. There is almost a total absence of self-generating movement for any kind of cause, save for an occasional slave rebellion. In view of the fact that the African American subculture has evidenced *mass passivity*, their twentieth century revolution becomes all the more remarkable.

When one contemplates the depth, the pervasiveness, and the tradition of prejudice and discrimination in America, the unique feature of the African

---

2   Rudolf Heberle, *Social Movements* (New York: Appleton-Century-Crofts, Incorporated, 1951), p. 23.

3   Herbert Blumer, *Collective Behavior,* in *New Outlines of the Principles of Sociology*, edited by Alfred McClung Lee (New York: Barnes and Nobles, 1951), p. 199.

4   Rudolf Heberle, *Observations on the Sociology of Social Movements, American Sociological Review*, XIV (1949), 349.

5   C. Wendell King, *Social Movements in the United States* (New York: Random House, 1964), p. 27.

American protest movement of the 1960's is the dearth of physical violence it has evoked. Direct confrontation with the laws, mores, and customs of the political system is dangerous because this technique actually challenges the legitimacy of the system itself. Yet the African American movement has been content to work within the existing framework of the political system and use only legitimate channels to realize its goals and objectives. With very few exceptions, modern African American civil rights organizations have aimed at acceptance by the existing politico-economic system. Direct action was utilized only after judicial and political approaches proved ineffective to their demands. Utilization of the existing political system, with all its liabilities, could very well be the outstanding feature of America's "unfinished revolution."

The following pages of this chapter will be structured in such a way as to allow the reader to examine the development of a social movement. After defining and itemizing the characteristics, the various types of movements will be discussed. In addition, factors conducive to the growth of movements, as well as social movement cycles, will be identified. The chapter will terminate with a brief discussion on social movement components.

Distinguishing Characteristics of Social Movements

Social movements develop as a result of unrest. They receive their motivating impetus from dissatisfaction with the status quo and from a desire for a new way of life, a new form of existence. The incredibility of a majority of the goals a social movement establishes is part of the campaign against the present state of affairs.

The path of a social movement characterizes the development of a new social order. In its embryonic stage, the movement offers only a poorly organized, amorphous body. Group behavior is rather primitive and the mechanisms of interaction are simple and voluntary. As a social movement emerges, it begins to take on the character of a society. Organization becomes concrete. A leadership hierarchy is structured and a corresponding division of labor is established. Customs and traditions come into being, and social rules and values emerge. Hence a subculture, a social organization, and a new scheme of life are developed.

Eric Hoffer maintained that there are a multitude of peculiarities common to all mass movements, be they religious, social, or nationalistic. The movements are not necessarily identical; however, there are specific characteristics which they mutually share and which give them very close approximation and affinity as a group.

1. All mass movements generate in their adherents a readiness to die and a proclivity for united action;
2. all of them, irrespective of the doctrine they preach and the program they project, breed fanaticism, enthusiasm, fervent hope, hatred and intolerance;
3. all of them are capable of releasing a powerful flow of activity in certain departments of life;
4. all of them demand blind faith and single-hearted allegiance;
5. all mass movements, however different in doctrine and aspiration, draw their early adherents from the same types of humanity; they all appeal to the same types of mind.[6]

Types of Social Movements

Numerous and varied are the categories under which social movements may be classified.[7] King employed three criteria for distinguishing types of movements: change, organization, and coordination.[8] Change may be either revolutionary, i.e. desiring a complete overthrow of an established social order, or reform, i.e. improving or amending what is wrong in the present social system, in nature. Although both seek to alter the social order and its existing institutions, there is a difference in the scope of the objectives of the two movements. A reform movement seeks to change some specific phase or limited area of the existing social order; it may seek, for example, to abolish child labor or to prohibit the consumption of alcohol. A revolutionary movement has a broader aim; it seeks to reconstruct the entire social order.

---

6   Eric Hoffer, *The True Believer* (New York: The New American Library of World Literature, Incorporated, 1963), p. 9.

7   According to Blumer, op. cit., pp. 199-218, social movements fall into three types: general, specific, and expressive. Arnold Green dichotomized movements into inclusive and segmented, in *Sociology, An Analysis of Life in Modern Society* (New York: McGraw-Hill Book Company, Incorporated, 1960), pp. 627-628; while Heberle, *Social Movements*, pp. 131-134, distinguished the following types of movements: the spiritual community, the following of a charismatic leader, and the utilitarian association between individuals.

8   King, op. cit., pp. 27-30.

Not only do the two types of movements differ in scope of their objectives, but also they attack from different vantage points. A reform movement works within the existing framework of society, therefore it accepts society's customs and conventions. Consequently, it becomes almost immune from criticism because it attacks social defects by employing the existing mores. On the other hand, a revolutionary movement proposes a new order of moral values by challenging the vogue mores. Quite naturally it is vulnerable to attack.

By seeking to realize its goals within the existing framework of a society, a reform movement has respectability and legitimacy. Because it accepts the present social order, with some modifications, it can employ existing institutions in attempting to reach its goals. In contrast, a revolutionary movement is prevented from utilizing societal institutions because, by very definition, it seeks to destroy them in their current form.

In attaining their goals, different tactics are used by the two movements. A reform movement attempts to carry out its aims by mobilizing a public opinion favorable disposed to its goals. As a result, it focuses its attention on a specific public issue and utilizes the discussion process. The procedure a revolutionary movement follows is the antithesis of this. Instead of attempting to mold public opinion, it makes every effort to create converts.

Because the goals of the two movements are different, their adherents will come from different strata of society. A reform movement tries to penetrate the ranks of the middle class public and arouse within it a vicarious compassion for the deprived group; while a revolutionary group carries its agitation into the lower echelons of society, the subcultures of distress and exploitation. It swells its membership ranks by bringing these people into the fold. As a result, it is usually oriented to the lower classes.

A social movement may be typed on the basis of its structure and organization. Organization, being a "more-or-less" characteristic, can best be explained by means of a continuum. At one end are such fraternal orders as the Knights of Columbus, the Shriners, et al. Here the rank order of positions is rigidly structured; more aggressive members work toward obtaining a variety of "degrees," various and sundry titles are conferred, rituals and ceremonies are elaborate, and policy matters are handled according to well-established rules. At the other end of the continuum movements have a very loose organizational structure, such as the Congress of Racial Equality. Here leaders are few and far between, ritual is absent or at best primitive, policy issues are settled as they arise rather than on any predetermined guidelines.

Coordination is still another component by which movements may be categorized. Technically, coordination refers to the harmonious adjustment of divergent parts. As the term is employed here, it means that unique function of organization whereby the chapters of multiunit movements are associated and linked together not only by singleness of purpose, but also by their mutual endeavors to promote that purpose. For example, CORE has as its primary goal the abolition of racial discrimination through techniques of non-violent direct action. Consequently, the degree of coordinated interaction among the several chapters of this multiunit movement may ultimately spell the success or failure of the implementation of its desired proposals.

Nature of Social Movements

According to Robert S. Lynd, in his "Introduction" in *Agrarian Socialism*, no phenomenon is more urgently in need of study today than the conditions under which new social movements may emerge in our society.

> ...Man's fate in societies living by big technology, urbanization, and division of labor is from now on a collective one. But social atomism has deeply corrupted our capacity to live together; and both personally and collectively our helplessness grows as democracy wanes. The recovery of democracy, if indeed it can occur, can happen only through men thinking together of what it is they want and organizing to move together.[9]

A discussion of the plethora of agents that account for the development of social movements will now be undertaken. There is a readily apparent dichotomy in the factors that cause growth between internal and external components. Every social movement occurs in a social context which has two primary and interrelated dimensions: the structure of society, with all its subsequent ramifications; and the culture, which encompasses the norms and values of a polity.

Cultural confusion is an inherent component of the mass society. With a variety of subgroups within the larger whole, there is quite naturally a diversity of codes of conduct, governing values, and systems of belief. This divergency of norms is axiomatic of contemporary existence.

Within the mass society there are very few, if any, absolutes on which all of the community will agree.

---

9   S. M. Lipset, *Agrarian Socialism: The Cooperative Commonwealth Federation in Saskatchewan*, Introduction by Robert S. Lynd (Berkeley and Los Angeles: University of California Press, 1950), p. vii.

...Our own culture has been in a state of unusual confusion at least since the beginning of the depression in 1929...The net result is that a uniformity of standards in regard to many questions concerning political, social, or economic life is, in our culture at the present time, the exception rather than the rule.[10]

Robert Merton has branded those cultural elements and sanctioning agencies that fail to contribute toward the cohesion of society dysfunctional.[11]

Thus ambiguous norms, cultural paradoxes, organizations with different ends working for power supremacy, and rapid change all contribute to the instability and inconsistency of a mass society. Cultural confusions spawn an atmosphere that nourishes even the most ludicrous of schemes. Moreover, many of these proposals actually prosper and grow.

Although it may seem paradoxical, another factor that spurs the growth of a social movement is cultural consistency. More specifically, if a movement is to be accepted it must have some compatibility with the society's general culture. Attention must be concentrated on the goals of the movement in ascertaining whether or not it is inharmonious with the existing culture.

> One of the most serious errors made in analyzing communism is that of focusing attention on the formal program of the party, so that it is assumed to be a partial fulfillment of the party's propaganda goals to create sentiment for unionization or similar "immediate" objectives. In fact, however, the significant partial goals are two kinds: the promotion of current propaganda objectives of interest to the Soviet Union..., and, equally important but less well understood, the inculcation of attitudes which neutralize the opposition to communism and create a favorable atmosphere for open community activity.[12]

Obviously, simple scrutiny of the goals of the Communists would show them to be inconsistent with the culture of America as we know it today.

Cultural drift, the process "where minor alterations slowly change the character and form of a way of life, but where the continuity of the event is

---

10　Hadley Cantril, *The Psychology of Social Movements* (New York: John Wiley and Son, Incorporated, 1941), p. 10.

11　Robert K. Merton, *Social Theory and Social Structure* (Glencoe, Illinois: Free Press, 1957), p. 51.

12　Philip Selznick, *The Organizational Weapon: A Study of Bolshevik Strategy and Tactics* (New York: McGraw-Hill Book Company, 1952), p. 188.

apparent,"[13] can facilitate the progress of a social movement. A movement can easily become the vanguard of drifts or tendencies already under way in some areas of the culture. Consequently, it merely becomes the personification of what society is slowly coming to regard as necessary. This creates a perplexing situation because what appears to be a liability is, in reality, an asset. All of the goals of a movement are not going to be compatible with society's traditional values; hence, the emergence of conflict. However, this conflict can be a blessing in disguise because modification of these values, in some form, may be unavoidable and even necessary for the proper functioning of society. Belief in free education, extension of the franchise, the constantly increasing prestige of science, and belief in equal civil rights for all are examples of cultural drifts in our own society.

Social heterogeneity is another contributory condition that increases the proliferation of social movements. A society made up of a series of diverse segments is bound to reflect this composition through a multiplicity of codes of conduct, customs, and values. An old cliché has it that the only thing Americans agree on is that they disagree. As a result, such American universals as democracy, capitalism, monotheism, and belief in the strength and capabilities of the individual are the subject of considerable discourse and debate, not only as to interpretation, but also as to worth and value. Conflict is bound to arise among those human beings who are trying to realize different goals and conflicting interests. If a society were homogeneous, a social movement could never develop because the demands of persons and groups would be fully satisfied. If demands are fully satisfied, there is no reason to fight the *system*.

According to Cantril, "a frame of reference is based on certain standards of judgment, and… an attitude emerges when a given situation is appraised by means of a frame of reference."[14] As a result, the ideology and program of a movement must have meaning for the populace, i.e. they must make sense to the recipients, or the movement will be ignored. Meaning that is successfully perceived greatly enhances the growth potential of any social movement. However, due to the fact that the goals of social movements are often interpreted for prospective adherents by present members, failure to comprehend their meaning is seldom an impediment to their acceptance.

---

13   Melville J. Herskovits, *Man and His Works* (New York: Alfred A. Knopf, 1949), p. 581.

14   Cantril, op. cit., p. 21.

Social structure is another contributory condition having significant importance for the success or failure of a social movement. Ralph Linton[15] felt that the prestige level at which a new element enters society has a direct correlation with its chances for success because it identifies the segment of the population who will accept it. If a social movement is identified with a specific socio-economic stratum, social rank is bound to determine which subculture in the community will respond enthusiastically and which will react adversely. For example, the Black Muslims continue to emphasize their affiliation with the working class. "Recruitment for the Movement is still predominately from among low-income groups at the lower end of the educational scale."[16] Obviously, the low level of esteem held for African Americans at the bottom of the economic pyramid seriously effects the establishment of a broad basis of support for the Black Muslims among all strata of society. There are those who feel that a movement will more readily be accepted if it is associated with individuals who are held in higher respect than with those who are dismissed or loathed.

The marginal utility of a social movement, that is the additional satisfaction one receives when the goals of the movement are reached, is still another component that can alter the whole course of the movement. Those individuals who are likely to derive benefits from a movement are likely to join it or at least be favorably disposed toward it, whereas those who have had a stake in things as they are ("a vested interest in the status quo") are likely to receive inconvenience from the movement, and hence may vigorously oppose it.

Individual discontent, with all its ramifications, becomes important to the development of a social movement when enough persons channel their efforts in some cause so as to give meaning to their dissatisfactions. Although the causes of discontent are numerous and varied, it is the effects of such discontent that are of special relevance to this study. Discontent fosters an eager reception for suggestion in the mind of the individual, a craving for meaning and value, and a desire for substitutes. Green has pointed out:

> Most leaders and followers of social movements are not neurotic; they are not self-paralyzed; they are not incapable of sustained personal action and sustained cooperation. Most of them are, however, afflicted with personality conflict in some degree… Theirs is a wide gap between aspiration and

---

15 Ralph Linton (editor), *Acculturation in Seven American Indian Tribes* (New York: D. Appleton-Century Company, Incorporated, 1940), p. 473.

16 C. Eric Lincoln, *The Black Muslims in America* (Boston: Beacon Press, 1963), p. 24.

achievement… The social movement they join always promises to recapture for them that which has been lost.[17]

The desire for change can serve as a strong stimulus to the growth of social movements. Many of those who enlist behind the banner of a growing revolutionary movement do so because they feel that such activity will lead to a hasty and dramatic change in their present existence. It should be mentioned here that discontent, operating by itself, does not create a desire for change. If men are going to undertake the arduous task of immense change:

> …they must be intensely discontented yet not destitute, and they must have the feeling that by the possession of some potent doctrine, infallible leader or some new technique they have access to a source of irresistible power. They must also have an extravagant conception of the prospects and potentialities of the future. Finally, they must be wholly ignorant of the difficulties involved in their vast undertaking.[18]

Contemporary communications, such as television, radio, and the press, play a role in social movement maturation. They either confuse the individual via a vast assortment of conflicting messages and send him off in quest of meaning or increase his desire for meaning by enlarging his awareness of what is transpiring in his environment and relive his sense of confusion by answering his questions and offering material for the solution of problems. In addition, present-day communication facilities enable leaders to reach the public and carry their messages to potential converts otherwise not available. Modern mass media thus serve as a bridge between mass society, on the one hand, and the growth of social movements, on the other.

The internal composition of a social movement can also affect its rate of growth. The goals of a movement must be realistic, fluid, and obtainable. They must contain the power to satisfy human wants if they are to favorably induce persons to join the movement. The means employed to realize the goals are the internal features that have a vital bearing on the fate of the movement. Ideology, organization and status system, group cohesion, and tactics are all components of a social movement that can encourage or discourage potential converts, depending upon their employment. (Since these concepts will be elaborated upon in a later section, no discussion of their characteristics or functions will be undertaken at this time.)

---

17   Green, op. cit., p. 625.
18   Hoffer, op. cit., p. 13.

It is quite possible to identify approximate stages in the development of a movement, assuming, of course, that it does not disintegrate before it reaches the stage of formal organization. It should be recalled that social movements do not develop a broad basis of support or, for that matter, even limited acceptance overnight. Rather than a spontaneous outburst, change is really the result of an incubation procedure. In essence, it is a process that advances, slowly or rapidly, depending on circumstances, over a period of time.

Carl Dawson and Warner Gettys[19] have offered one schematic framework of four stages: the stage of social unrest, the stage of popular excitement, the stage of formalization, and the stage of institutionalization.[20]

Initial conditions of discontent, dissatisfaction, and other vexations of the spirit must be present if a social movement is to be launched. Social changes, destruction of perceived rules and statuses, and norm and value alterations sow the seeds of mass dissatisfaction. The populous becomes vulnerable to appeals that promise to alleviate their discontent. For example,

> ...Moral rearmament became a popular movement only when it began to tap the spiritual anguish of religious upper-middle-class people who saw all they had lived and hoped for threatened by various nationalistic and socialistic uprisings.[21]

Agitation for mobilization purposes plays a significant role at this stage, although there is almost a total absence of formal organization and discipline. Individuals and groups are looking for a purpose and channels of access to implement their desired aims. Portions of the population are in a state of eager anticipation. The stage is set for a Moses to deliver them from evil and lead them into the Promised Land. However, much to everyone's chagrin, he has failed to materialize, or the small cadre of leaders that have developed are still so innocuous that they can hold no one's attention.

---

19 Carl A. Dawson and Warner E. Gerrys, *An Introduction to Sociology* (New York: The Ronald Press Company, 1929), Chapter XX.

20 Hoffer, op. cit., pp. 119-138, has portrayed three stages: (1) men of words, (2) the fanatics, and (3) the practical men of action. King, op. cit., pp. 40-57, has developed a comprehensive scheme that identifies the two dimensions of every social movement. Dimension one concerns itself with events within the movement (incipient, organizational, and stable phases), while the second dimension includes the movement's relations with the external social order (innovation, selection, and integration).

21 Green, op. cit., p. 628.

During the stage of popular excitement more precise concepts are developed to explain the adverse conditions people are confronted with and what can be done to alleviate the suffering. Goals and objectives are heightened. At this stage of growth the leader is more likely a soothsayer or reformer. Interest begins to be focused upon a *sorcerer-like* individual who can deliver the as yet informal membership.

A program of performance and platitudes to encourage the faithful emerge at this stage. Some semblance of organization develops. Branch or chapter proliferation begins to appear as several people who have heard the master return with the message and establish groups, clubs, and debating societies with themselves at the head. A spirit of invincibility begins to permeate throughout the movement. Members start to think of themselves as part of an overwhelming army that will eventually obliterate the forces of evil and wickedness.

As innovation threatens the status quo, opposition to the movement begins to surface and manifest itself. If the movement is sufficiently strong to withstand external assault, opposing forces will fail in their attempt to destroy it. If the forces which are endeavoring to impede the progress of the movement fail in their attempts to do so, they merely add stimulation to the movement's growth potential. The sacrosanct leader becomes a martyr, and his flock a group of embattled heroes. What is even more significant, the cause becomes vindicated as it has been maintained in the face of hostile censure and objection.

If the movement is not overpowered by such intervening variables as a potent opposition or apathetic respondents, it embarks upon the stage of formalization with all its subsequent ramifications: definite rules, policies, and goals; a concrete ideology; a chain of command organized on a line-and-staff basis; utilization of propaganda on a large scale; the development of discipline; and the employment of tactics for desired ends.

Survival at this stage is greatly enhanced if the movement has achieved some of its desired goals, or at least has made some observable strides that show promise of eventual success. Dedicated participation by the rank and file is not a perpetual thing. Moreover, formal organization increases the probability of internal dissension and discord. Consequently, the movement must produce if it is to survive.

Seldom is the institutional stage realized. If the movement has crystallized into a stable organization and has been incorporated as a fixture in the framework of society, it has reached the apex of its career. At this juncture, leadership is represented by the "administrator" rather than by the statesman who was in vogue during the organizational period. Most movements, even the triumphant ones, stabilize at the formal organizational stage. Labor unions and Methodism are examples of the elite groups that have become institutionalized.

Social Movement Components

The structural-functional aspects of social movements are extremely important because there is interest in determining the functions that are necessary to the survival of a movement and in identifying the structure(s) which performs these functions. With reference to social movements, structure is "the differentiation of roles and the distribution of power, influence, and authority within the movement."[22]

All social movements have an ultimate aim toward which they direct all their activities. Even though these goals may be explicit or covert, they are nevertheless always present in one form or another in every movement. In addition, most movements employ both general and specific goals; the former enhance the malleability of the movement's organization and tactics and increase its broad basis of support, while the latter increase its appeal to the specific interests in society. Goals which are practical, flexible, realizable, and utilitarian cannot insure the success of a social movement, but they can certainly facilitate its progress. The absence of these goal characteristics would be reflected in the movement's probable lack of achievement.

The vast array of ideas, doctrines, theories, mores, values, and strategic and tactical methods that are indicative of a movement constitute what is known as the ideology of the movement. To be more precise, the following items seem to be present in every ideology:

1. a statement of the objective, purpose, and premises of the movement;
2. a body of criticism and condemnation of the existing structure which the movement is attacking and seeking to change;
3. a body of defensive doctrine which serves as a justification of the movement and of its objectives;
4. a body of belief dealing with policies, tactics, and practical operation of the movement;
5. the myths of the movement.[23]

---

22 Heberle, *Social Movements*, p. 15.
23 Blumer, op. cit., p. 210.

An ideology is to a social movement what a platform is to a political party: it explains the movement in terms of its objectives. Normally, a portion of it is technical, intellectual, and esoteric in an attempt to gain respectability among the academic elite. On the other hand, in order to appeal to the masses, the ideology has a side to it which is less than mundane. In this role, ideology relies more on emotion than on reason to accomplish its goals. Stereotypes, glittering generalities, shibboleths, and folk arguments are very much in vogue. The movement's principles are presented in such a way as to make for immediate comprehension and digestion. Unless an ideology has both prestige and popular appeal, it will contribute very little, if anything, to the success of the movement.

Group cohesion and esprit de corps are essential ingredients if a social movement is to hold together and survive. Basically, cohesion gives the movement continuance. If internal dissension and dissatisfaction ever hold sway in a social movement, it is headed for oblivion. Esprit de corps (the prevailing spirit of a collective body) contributes to social movements by fostering feelings of intimacy and brotherhood which encourage cooperation rather than personal competition, and by reinforcing the individual's sense of belonging to the group a feeling of collective support is established.

If a social movement is to be successful, some degree of organization is absolutely imperative. The greater the magnitude of the group, the more sophisticated the organization needed. If a chain of command is established whereby leaders and led are designated, the movement is organized. Organization consists of arranging parts in an interdependent fashion. Each segment has a special relation with respect to the whole. Specific individuals are given definite powers and duties pertinent to the functioning of the group. These people can issue commands and expect compliance with their requests on the part of their members. The degree of organization is correlated with the functions of the movement. In addition, the more elaborate the form of organization, the more structural the elements that will be created; i.e. a bureaucracy or *staff* will aid the leaders in performing their duties, and a constitution and by-laws will be initiated in order that the activities of all members may be regulated.

All organized movements need financial resources if they are to carry on their activities. Funds can be raised in many ways: dues, contributions, special assessments, donations from the parent organization, special benefits, and revenue from the sale of organizational articles or from enterprises controlled by the movement. The class position of the membership of the movement generally will determine how it goes about its fund raising chores. Those organizations that represent the upper-middle class and wealthy strata of our society (the Junior League, cultural clubs, et. al.) can readily be financed by voluntary contributions. However, those representing the moderate to lower economic echelons of our culture (like CORE) will have to rely upon dues and assessments.

The very existence of a social movement necessitates a differentiation between leaders and followers.[24] Leadership has many facets and many moods, although the leader himself cannot manufacture the conditions which allow a movement to grow and prosper. Actually it seems as though the leader really capitalizes upon the conditions that produce a social movement.

> There is a period of waiting in the wings—often a very long period—for all the great leaders whose entrance on the scene seems to us a most crucial point in the course of a mass movement. Accidents and the activities of other men have to set the stage for them before they can enter and start their performance. "The commanding man in a momentous day seems only to be the last accident in a series."[25]

Legal leaders derive their power and authority from the office they hold rather than from any personal qualities. On the other hand, the charismatic leader possesses power and authority by virtue of his own unique characteristics. On many occasions he is not only the movement's leader but also its founder. While few, if any, leaders are all legal or all charismatic, the probability is great that they belong in one of these two categories.

In addition to the leader, a movement also has the bureaucrat and the agitator in its executive hierarchy. Organizational functionaries who are more than members but less than supreme leaders constitute what is known as the bureaucracy. The individual in this in-between group of organization is known as the bureaucrat. His functions are basically administrative, as he carries out the directives of the leader and supervises and controls the activities of the rank and file. The agitator might be stylized as the *cheer leader* of a social movement. His primary contribution is made in the initial stages of the movement, as it is here that his promotional and proselytizing efforts swell the membership ranks. The agitator sows the seeds of ferment among a population by indoctrinating it with new ideas and visions that

---

24   For an illumination discussion of leaders and sub leaders see Sigmund Neuman, *Permanent Revolution* (New York: Harper and Brothers, 1942), Chapters II and III.

25   Hoffer, op. cit., p. 104.

make it dissatisfied with its present lot and circumstances. In addition, an agitator can also play a vital role as the director of nonviolent direct action if a movement employs such tactics in attempting to reach its goals. In reality, these three functionaries may overlap and play continuous roles instead of each engaging in only one discrete type.

Tactics refer to the science and art of employing the use of forces in battle, while strategy encompasses the science and art of employing battles to secure the objects of war. As far as social movements are concerned, strategy and tactics refer to the methods by which they seek to realize their goals. The type of tactic used in a particular environment is entirely dependent upon both the nature of the situation and the social order in which the movement is functioning. Inappropriate tactics can destroy a movement, as potential members may be alienated. Moreover, the state, which has a monopoly on the legitimate use of force, may decide that the tactics constitute a menace to society, therefore the movement should be outlawed. Tactics really depend on the estimate of the situation at hand. They are dynamic, fluid, and variable. They take form from the nature of conditions, the urgency of the circumstances, and the resourcefulness of the people.

Lack of concern for the personal sacrifices that each member has to make in order that desired goals can be realized is the chief characteristic of a social movement. The personal self must be lost in the corporate whole. Thus a person will prostrate himself for a social movement, as long as he never feels alone and can identify with a collective whole.

A tight interrelationship exists between how each member perceives the movement and his motivation in joining and continuing as a member. Consideration will now be given to one of the omniferous classifications of types of social movement adherents.[26]

H. G. Barnett[27] has developed a classification of four types of individuals who, he felt, are the potential acceptors of innovations: (1) the dissident, (2)

---

26   Hoffer, op. cit., pp. 29-56, felt that the discarded and rejected are more often than not the building blocks of a country's future. As a result, he used the following categories for his classifications of the disaffected: (1) the poor, (2) misfits, (3) the inordinately selfish, (4) the ambitious facing unlimited opportunities, (5) minorities, (6) the bored, and (7) the sinners. King, op. cit., pp. 60-66, has made a few panoramic observations about the types of people who are receptive to new ideas, and hence lend themselves well to the membership ranks of social movements. His analytical frameworks includes biographical determinates, the role of crisis, and member motives.

27   H. G. Barnett, *Innovation: The Basis of Cultural Change* (New York: McGraw-

the indifferent, (3) the disaffected, and (4) the resentful. The dissident is the one who plays the role of an *iceberg*, so to speak. On the surface he appears to accept society's norms and values. However, penetrating the individual's veneer, it is found that he consistently objects to some conventions his group supports. The indifferent person is one who is full of ambivalence. He does not necessarily chastise conventions; on the other hand, he is not dedicated to their support. The disaffected exhibit, at least temporarily, hostility to conventions they once lent their support to. Their analysis of the current situation will determine whether or not they accept the new or retain the old. In any society there will be, almost without exception, more *have nots* than *haves*. Hence, enter the resentful, who form the envious component of the milieu and who feel that a change or alteration might prove advantageous to them. As a result, they are receptive to proposals and suggestions.

The above categories of potential adherents to social movements are not, of course, all-inclusive. Their purpose is to isolate reasonably stable and observable classes that exist over time in society, regardless of the contemplated change or changes and the instruments employed for carrying it or them out. One cannot completely overlook the fact that the type of change and the organization formulated for carrying it out may encourage an enthusiastic response on the part of people not falling into the aforementioned categories. However, when it is remembered that only a minority in any society become members of social movements, the previously listed categories at least aid in understanding the types of personalities who join social movements.

The barometer of dissatisfaction within a society's social order is the rise of a social movement. Discontent develops when people feel that society's norms and values are no longer paragons which should be emulated by everyone. Social solidarity is the product of agreement by all on social values and norms. If the basic values and fundamental norms of society are not accepted by all groups, a peaceful social order is impossible and then society's "sense of community" will be endangered. Into this vacuum enters the social movement whose desire is to alter the social order in such a way as to relieve the group's distress and anxiety over their contemporary situation. Depending upon how soon sufficient and well-timed reforms in social institutions are implemented, a social movement will either advance or disintegrate.

Hill Book Company, Incorporated, 1953), pp. 378-410.

CHAPTER III

The Congress Of Racial Equality: Prototype Of A Civil Rights Organization

○ ○

As long as there are social organizations that produce men who do not accept the status quo, who see "the inhumanity of man to man" as a crime, there will be hope in the human race.[1]

The primary focus of this chapter will be on a case study of the local chapter of CORE. National CORE will be discussed first in order to establish a frame of reference by which the local unit can be viewed. The philosophy of nonviolent direct action will be treated at length because it is primarily responsible for constructing the patterns that the African American protest took. The Los Angeles chapter of CORE will then be described, analyzed, and evaluated by means of the following organizational indices: goals, government and organization, meetings, membership recruitment and socialization, finances, physical plant, symbolism, publications, and direct action tactics.

The Founding of the National Congress of Racial Equality

In 1941 James Farmer discovered one of the unique paradoxes of the African American subculture: while knowing that *Jim Crow* was detrimental to the African American's development and subsequent advancement, the African American community nevertheless was actually supporting it. Determined

---

1   S. M. Lipset, *Agrarian Socialism: The Cooperative Commonwealth Federation in Saskatchewan* (Berkley and Los Angeles: University of California Press, 1950), p. 286.

to alter this situation, he constructed a memorandum acknowledging this condition and suggesting that a tenacious body of individuals form an organization that would employ personal nonviolent direct action to terminate discrimination and segregation.

Although the memorandum was widely disseminated among liberals, pacifists, socialists, and student and religious organizations, one interracial group, composed for the most part of University of Chicago students, was especially responsive. Having been refused service at a small restaurant near the university, they attempted negotiations with the management. Their efforts met with failure, even though Illinois law forbids racial discrimination. Consequently, they *sat-in*.

> ...We really bollixed that place for a day. It was a small place, and when we sat at the tables we filled all the seats. Finally, the lady who owned it broke down and served us.[2]

In order to continue to carry out demonstrations, a permanent organization was established. The Committee of Racial Equality, as it was originally called, was committed to the use of nonviolent direct action for ending discrimination in all its sundry forms. News of CORE's activities began to circulate to other areas, and a conference was called in Chicago in June, 1943, to establish a nationwide organization. To direct this loose federation of autonomous local groups a national chairman, James Farmer, was elected. In 1944, at the second national conference in Detroit, the organization's name was changed to the present one, the Congress of Racial Equality.

Initially, CORE chapters were college-centered, and most of them were small in size for the simple reason that very few people were willing to make the mandatory sacrifices of time, energy, and reputation. Small though the chapters were, they were nevertheless all-encompassing. As a result, the leadership and membership of CORE chapters contained people from all segments of society.

CORE's original chapters were situated in the Northern states and devoted most of their time to integrating public accommodations. Gradually, CORE began to penetrate the border states of Maryland, Missouri, and Oklahoma. However, the concept of direct action was not successfully applied in the entire South until the middle of the 1950's.

---

2   Martin Mayer, "Core: The Shock Troops of the African American Revolt," *Post*, November 21, 1964, p. 79.

CORE's first chapters were largely middle class. Triumphant attempts to obtain positions in semiskilled employment capacities increased the number of working class African Americans in the organization and discretely altered the character of the significantly white, middle class Northern units. On the other hand, from the outset Southern chapters had a high percentage of African Americans.

Slowly, but surely, CORE began to expand the scope of its chapters and operations. It should be emphasized, however, that this was an evolutionary and not a revolutionary process. At the outset there were no salaried staff members. During this period the Fellowship of Reconciliation allowed CORE a little free office space. Obviously, these were CORE's lean years. Nevertheless, a few chapters made significant contributions to the cause of civil rights. CORE units in St. Louis and Baltimore, for example, saw to it that lunch counter discrimination on a citywide level was terminated permanently. The close of the 1950's saw CORE develop into a cohesive group of strong chapters and trained staff members.

Two events in the 1960's marked the emergence of CORE as a mature force in the African American struggle for equal opportunity for all and thrust the organization into the national spotlight. During the sit-ins in Greensboro, North Carolina, the New York office of CORE received a call from Dr. George Simpkins, president of the local branch of the National Association for the Advancement of Colored People (NAACP), requesting assistance for the students. Responding immediately, CORE sent field workers to Greensboro to carry on workshops for those students interested in nonviolent direct action. In addition, CORE officials carried on discussions at the national level, with the dime store chains involved in the sit-ins. The result of all this activity was firmly to entrench CORE in the upper regions of the South and to develop a broad basis of support for the organization throughout the nation.

Even more significant than the sit-ins were the freedom rides through the South, which tested this area's disposition to comply with the Supreme Court's rulings on integration of bus terminals in interstate commerce. The story of the freedom rides is really the story of James Farmer, CORE's national director.

Farmer became a trade union organizer in 1946 and was absent from the civil rights movement until 1959, when he was hired by the NAACP to be its national program director. Two years later, on February 1, 1961, at the age of forty, James Farmer became national director of CORE. He transformed this federation of local units into the *shock troops* of the African American revolt, and the freedom rides helped him do it. Contrary to popular belief, the first freedom ride (called the Journey of Reconciliation) took place in 1947, under the co-sponsorship of the Fellowship of Reconciliation and of CORE,[3] to test the outlawing of segregation in interstate travel. When this journey was over there were no reporters present to query the riders as to whether or not the trip was beneficial. The scene was quite different fourteen years later.

On May 1, 1961 thirteen freedom riders—six white and seven African American, including James Farmer—assembled at Fellowship House in Washington for training. Three days later they departed, this time to test the desegregation of all facilities used by interstate passengers outside the actual vehicles. Moreover, the freedom ride would penetrate to the epicenter of the Deep South.[4]

When the rides were finally over, the objective was accomplished. The Interstate Commerce Commission issued an order forbidding segregated terminal facilities in interstate commerce. Over and above the desired victory was the final emergence of CORE as the most resolute and creative organization in the civil rights arena.

Consider what has transpired in CORE's life since the freedom rides. For the past five years it has nearly doubled both its membership and its budget. For the fiscal year ending May 31, 1959 CORE had income totaling $62,000, while May 31, 1964 saw it take in $900,000. (In the interests of objectivity, it should be mentioned that today CORE, like other civil rights organizations, is facing financial difficulties. CORE now owes $150,000; in addition, its leadership hierarchy had to serve without pay during much of early 1965. It has had to cancel plans to open a new Washington office, and is cutting costs by not replacing staff members who quit.)[5] Presently, over 80,000 people belong to CORE; this places it second only to the NAACP in terms of membership. Other statistics are equally impressive. That CORE is a nationwide organization is attested to by the fact that it now has 124 affiliated chapters in every geographical section of America.[6] Its professional staff now includes 137 individuals, whereas it only had seven in 1959. The

3   For an illuminating discourse on this freedom ride, and the 1961 freedom ride, see James Peck, *Freedom Ride* (New York: Grove Press, Incorporated, 1962).

4   For a day-by-day report of the nightmare the freedom riders underwent see the Southern Regional Council Report as synthesized by Louis E. Lomax, *The African American Revolt* (New York: The New American Library of World Literature, Incorporated, 1963), pp. 147-156.

5   "Pinched Purses," *Time*, LXXXV (February 12, 1965), 17.

6   At Durham, North Carolina, during CORE's 1965 annual convention, the announcement of sixteen new chapters was made, bringing the total to 140.

genius of CORE leadership is its flexibility and fluidity. It operates along the lines of *management by crisis*. It is forever engaged in spot planning, and rapid implementation of such planning.

What about the followers of this organization? Probably the most significant characteristic to note is the alteration in the social class of the adherents. In its embryonic stage, CORE chapters were groups of strongly devoted intellectuals. Today, the organization cuts across class lines and has truly become a mass movement.

One NAACP official has described CORE's membership as "a bunch of loony birds and crackpots."[7] At first glance it would appear that the statement had some substance because a number of CORE members have been associated with pacifist, socialist, and antiwar groups. Closer scrutiny, however, also reveals the fact that such personages as Tallulah Bankhead, Helen Hayes, and Eleanor Roosevelt have been or are enlisted in the ranks of CORE. Being an activist organization that utilizes the streets rather than the courtroom, CORE naturally draws its supporters from the more aggressive, action-oriented people in our society. Consequently, it is susceptible to criticism.

The success of CORE's activities in the 1960's has brought thousands of new members into the fold and has enabled multitudes of ordinary people to take part in the fight against discrimination. Growth, however, has also been accompanied by problems, one of which deserves our brief attention. A number of the new devotees are not familiar with the philosophical teachings of Mahatma Gandhi as implemented by CORE in the form of nonviolent direct action. "Their very number has made it difficult to train them in the methods and in the philosophy of nonviolent direct action."[8] Rule of Action number six states that a member "will meet the anger of any individual or group in the spirit of good will and creative reconciliation: he will submit to assault and will not retaliate in kind either by act or word."[9] When one views the derogatory placards present at CORE actions, the taunting of law enforcement officials, and the vindictive attitude toward the "man," it seems as though the spirit of good will has not endured with the proliferation of the movement. The fatal result of this situation is the inability to mobilize a favorable public opinion that will be responsive to CORE's demands.

---

7   "Races: Confused Crusade," *Time*, LXXIX (January 12, 1962), 15.

8   Marvin Rich, *The Congress of Racial Equality and Its Strategy, The Annals of the American Academy of Political and Social Science*, CCCLVII (January, 1965), 117.

9   CORE, *CORE Rules for Action* (New York: CORE, 1963), p.4.

Annual conventions are held by CORE. The National Advisory committee (consisting of such distinguished personalities are Martin Luther King, Walter Reuther, and Lillian Smith) offers advice and assistance, while the routine day-to-day planning is handled by the National Action Council, which also has the power to make policy decisions between conventions if they are necessary. Working within the framework of the Constitution and the Rules for Action, these groups take charge of the development and policy of national CORE.

As outlined by the organization itself, national CORE is responsible for the following activities:

(1) Maintains a national office, and a field staff to stimulate organization of new groups and to encourage the growth of established locals.

(2) Publishes literature of two types: (1) material for the use of its groups (such as the Organizational Manual); and (2) pamphlets of wider interest on race relations, usually involving nonviolent direct action (such as Martin Luther King's pamphlet on the Montgomery bus protest).

(3) Publishes the *CORElator*, to give wider circulation to action stories of local groups and of projects (such as the Freedom Rides) sponsored by National CORE itself.

(4) Serves as a clearing house for its local groups, setting up Training Conferences and Conventions where the locals may interchange problems and solutions involving action and organizational practices.

(5) Represents CORE on a national level.

(6) Sponsors training programs such as action workshops and national action projects. [10]

Today, as in the past, CORE remains basically a Northern movement. Only twenty-four of its 124 chapters are in the old states of the Confederacy. Elementary qualification standards allow almost any group desiring membership to become affiliated with CORE. Groups as small as ten members are eligible if they are noncommunist, accept the tenets of nonviolence, and have the ability to demonstrate. Low requirements have their effect, as witness the poor financial standing, shabby physical plant, and almost nonexistent staffs of nearly every local chapter.

The majority of CORE's work is carried on by its chapters. Semiautonomous, they vary in structure according to the different problems

10   CORE, *This Is CORE* (New York: CORE, n.d.), pp.6-7.

confronting them in the various environments they serve. Nevertheless, they all have a number of traits in common:

(1) Weekly or bi-weekly membership meetings to carry on business, approve action project plans, etc.
(2) Executive or Steering Committee to predigest some discussions before the membership meetings. Some groups have Special Action Units or Committees which serve this function in setting up projects.
(3) Membership Committee to recruit, orient, and screen applicants for membership and make recommendations to the General Membership Meeting for final approval.
(4) The usual organizational officers, including chairman, vice chairman, recording secretary, corresponding secretary, treasurer and financial secretary. [11]

In an effort to prevent the loss of another generation of school children to apathy and resentment, CORE recently has moved into the African American ghetto. By canvassing door-to-door in these blighted areas, CORE is able to ascertain what these people need and desire. It follows this up with programs to improve housing, educational and recreational facilities, the number of registered voters, and employment opportunities. By employing nonviolent direct action in the African American's back yard, CORE hopes to alleviate some of the race's chronic suffering and to develop potent community organization. Already a number of CORE Community Centers, institutions devoted to study, teaching, and recreation, have sprung up in Mississippi, Louisiana, and Florida.

Working in the ghettos naturally destroys much of CORE's romanticism. Many of the organization's adherents could fall away, as they originally joined in the hope of engaging in activities far different from those which have now been outlined for them. However, the law of life is change, and CORE must change in order to meet new situations and new problems if it is to survive and be in the vanguard of the civil rights movement.

CORE Philosophy

In America the CORE technique of nonviolent direct action finally has matured as a tool for combating racial injustice. Its philosophical heritage is a diverse one, having its foundation in the teachings of a number of different

---

11   Ibid.. p.7.

prophets.   Its methods of procedure are based on those developed and employed by Gandhi to free India from the shackles of British rule.

Satyagraha, or the force which is born of truth and love or nonviolence, represents the emergence of a new social institution which employs a unique technique for solving conflicts of all natures. [12] Instead of relying on Machiavellian physical force and fraud, Satyagraha is structured around the force of love.   The roots of this ideology are sunk deep in the fertile soil of Indian culture.

The Indian contributions assisted in the development of the ideology of Satyagraha by offering such concepts as sacrifices, Ahimsa, non-injury, in thought, word, or deed to any breathing thing, a deep faith in the efficiency of nonviolent suffering self-imposed and borne personally, and love is stronger than revenge.   Christ's life and teachings were the epitome of nonviolent resistance, and they made a profound impression on the modern-day follower of Satyagraha, Mahatma Gandhi.   Because legitimate and parliamentary activity failed to achieve economic and political results in India, the way was cleared for a national program of direct action.   Gandhi's ideology of Satyagraha succeed in mobilizing the country's vast population behind his banner because his program rejuvenated the stagnant energies of an entire civilization.   His philosophy silenced the weapons of the British Empire and released the people from bondage.

How did he go about transforming this ideology into a *flesh and blood* movement that ultimately overcame the British Raj?   Satyagraha is based on the premise that the polity involved has a grievance that consumes almost every member of the community.   It is necessary that the grievance be of considerable magnitude or it will not lend itself to transformation in the form of a *cause* which can elicit sacrifice and suffering from the polity's members on its behalf.

Satyagraha can progress through a number of stages and forms in order to terminate the *cause* successfully (see Figure 1).   At first, negotiations with responsible parties and arbitration by a third party are always undertaken in an attempt to settle the conflict peacefully.   These activities supplement whatever legislative channels are open.   If all these steps fail the second stage in the program of non-violent direct action, agitation, is undertaken. Every effort is made to generate *cause-consciousness* among the population. It is hoped that the opposition will be influenced to yield by the aroused

---

12   Krishnalal Shridharani, *War Without Violence* (New York: Harcourt, Brace and Company, Incorporated, 1939).   Most of the material in this section is based upon this source.

population, on the one hand, and by the vicarious neutrals who are interested in the issue, on the other.

If the group's desires are still thwarted, the third stage of the program of nonviolent direct action is launched. *Cause-consciousness* is expressed in the form of demonstrations. Mass meetings, resolutions, and work stoppage are characteristic of this stage.

The Satyagrahis feel that nonviolence is always superior to violence. More specifically, the power a nonviolent person has at his disposal is much greater than the power he would have if he were violent. Even though moral suasion has failed, direct action is nonviolent, and not revolutionary, in nature. In order to justify the use of nonviolent direct action, self-purification is introduced as the fourth phase of Satyagraha. According to Gandhi, "nonviolence implies as complete self-purification as is humanly possible.[13]

---

13   M.K. Gandhi, *Non-Violence in Peace and War* (Ahmedbad: Navajivan Publishing House, 1949), p. 111.

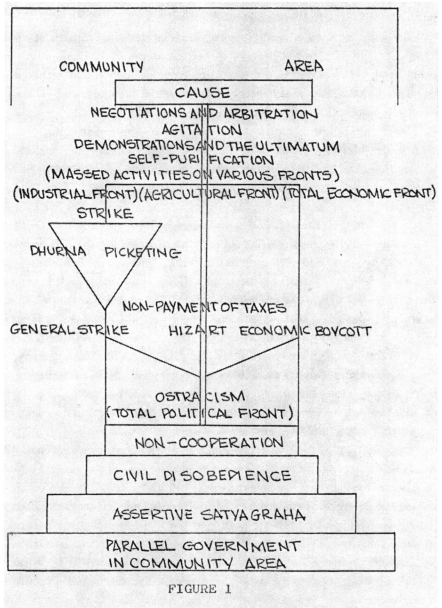

COMMUNITY   AREA

CAUSE

NEGOTIATIONS AND ARBITRATION
AGITATION
DEMONSTRATIONS AND THE ULTIMATUM
SELF-PURIFICATION
(MASSED ACTIVITIES ON VARIOUS FRONTS)
(INDUSTRIAL FRONT) (AGRICULTURAL FRONT) (TOTAL ECONOMIC FRONT)
STRIKE

DHURNA   PICKETING

NON-PAYMENT OF TAXES
GENERAL STRIKE   HIZART   ECONOMIC BOYCOTT

OSTRACISM
(TOTAL POLITICAL FRONT)

NON-COOPERATION

CIVIL DISOBEDIENCE

ASSERTIVE SATYAGRAHA

PARALLEL GOVERNMENT
IN COMMUNITY AREA

FIGURE 1

THE PATTERN OF A SUCCESSFUL SATYAGRAHA

The Satyagrahis feel that the injustices they are fighting against might not have occurred had they not been submissive. As a result, they begin to alter their own conduct and thinking, for if the populous no longer sins the government cannot live on its own wickedness.

In India, Satyagraha's self-purification phase has most often taken the forms of fasting and public prayers. America's *unfinished revolution*, on the other hand, has employed sit-ins, picketing, freedom rides, and mass marches as forms of self-purification. The type of wrong and the mores and values of the society determine the forms self-purification will take.

Satyagraha's chronological development is somewhat difficult to depict from here on because many of its forms are instruments rather than phases that develop one from the other. Yet a degree of continuity can be established. The strike is a lethal weapon that can be employed to hinder the operations of government, industries aligning themselves with and supporting the government, and government operated economic activities. One of the outgrowths of a strike is picketing. It increases the effectiveness of a strike by visually advertising it to the public. Dhurna, *the father of all sit-down strikes*, is the ultimate extension of striking and picketing. It is one of the most poignant ways of mobilizing public opinion because the populous is against violence in crushing strikes, and if it is not employed it is very difficult to force sit-down strikers to capitulate. Moreover, it often reaches many of the inert segments of a society and goads them into participating in the direct action. The economic boycott, whereby one group refrains from using or purchasing the products of facilities of another group, is a well-known weapon. Often it is accompanied by Swadeshi, which is a scheme of supporting native industries and of revitalizing cottage crafts.

The ninth stage of Satyagraha is nonpayment of taxes. This form of nonviolent direct action is illegal as it violates the laws of the state. Failure to pay taxes jeopardizes the government's ability to exist. The idea for this concept of Satyagraha came from the Boston transcendentalist, Henry David Thoreau. Arrested in 1846 for failing to pay the Massachusetts poll tax, he wrote the now classic essay "Civil Disobidience."[14] While it attracted little interest initially, its eventual acclaim lends credence to the platitude "the pen is mightier than the sword." His treatise became "Gandhi's source-book in the Indian campaign for Civil Resistance, and (it) has been read and pondered by thousands who hope to find some way to resist seemingly

14   Cited by Alpheus T. Mason and Richard H. Leach, *In Quest of Freedom* (Englewood Cliffs, New Jersey: Prentice-Hall, Incorporated, 1960), p.297.

irresistible force."[15] Thoreau felt that the way to destroy tyranny was through the employment of passive resistance which could take the form of failure to pay taxes, refusal to cooperate with the government, and, if need be, surrender to arrest and imprisonment.

A unique derivation of the failure to pay taxes is the concept known as Hizrat, which denotes mass emigration from the regions of oppression. A good example of this technique is the African American's *Back to Africa* campaign in the earlier portion of the present century, and the Black Muslim demand for a *Separate state* at the present time. The strength of this weapon comes from its ability to nullify the opposition's power. If there is no one to be governed, it is impossible to govern.

To a great many, nonviolence is unintelligible. However, it ceases to be esoteric when it is viewed as non-cooperation. "Political power, not resting on the willing and genuine consent of a vast majority of the people can only function, in the last resort, by the use of force and violence."[16] Consequently, if the people retract their support the political system must eventually cease to function. The difficulty in employing the weapon of non-cooperation is that it attains maximum results only when it mobilizes the bulk of the population to participate in the program. (Until very recently, inability to generate a vicarious response among the *crisis strata* was one of the primary problems of the African American movement.) Anyone who contributes to the maintenance of the state in any way is sinning because, once the decision is made not to cooperate with the system, the whole has to be rejected. Self-sacrifice and self-denial are the essential characteristics of non-cooperation. If it is not successful, failure will come from "poverty of response" rather than from any inherent weakness in the ideology.

Another technique of Satyagraha is ostracism, sometimes referred to as *social boycotting*. It is a practice whereby individuals who refuse to participate in the policy of non-cooperation as implemented against the system are excommunicated from their fellows. Normally, it is vindicated on the premise that by forming a *fifth column* and assisting the polity's foes he has relinquished whatever prerogatives he enjoyed as a member of the community. (In America this method has been used by labor union members

---

15   Henry Seidel Canby, *Thoreau* (Boston: Houghton Mifflin Company, 1939), p.235.

16   Gandhi, op. cit., pp.482-483.

when venting their animosities against the scabs.) The dissenter becomes "a political pariah beyond the pale of social intercourse."[17]

Civil disobedience, a more extreme form of direct action, takes the form of a *peaceful revolution* in that passive resistance rather than force of arms is resorted to in order to accomplish desired objectives. Because established state laws are broken, civil disobedience becomes extralegal in the culture. Quite naturally the government must arrest and imprison all violators of society's laws. However, by submitting willfully to punishment, the state's penal institutions are filled beyond capacity. As a result, these coercive agencies are neutralized.

In a desperate attempt to restore law and order, the state employs organized violence. Nowhere can this pattern be seen more vividly than during the African American demonstrations in Montgomery, Alabama. On March 16, 1965, 600 young protesters led by James Forman, executive secretary of SNCC, marched from the African American Alabama State College, situated about two miles from Montgomery, to within two blocks of the capitol, where they were stopped by city police. Refusing to disperse, they sat down in the street to wait it out, and were later joined by another group of about fifty persons. The second group departed when fifteen mounted deputies moved toward them with nightsticks and ropes. Then they turned on the larger group and employed clubs, canes, and ropes to route the 600 demonstrators. One college student was backed against the brick wall of a house and clubbed. Another horseman flailed demonstrators with a rope. When the melee was over, at least eight persons were injured and required hospital treatment. During the entire incident, however, the demonstrators refused to retaliate, and herein lies their strength. Not only are they able to bring the issue to the forefront of the consciences of the nation and arouse public opinion, but also their attackers begin to lose their desire to overwhelm helpless individual who abstain from offering any physical resistance.

> …The essence of the matter is not an appeal to violence, but an appeal to human decencies which in America are still but partially cloaked under various more formal ways of responding; and which can be easily aroused by dramatization of direct action.[18]

Like a victorious political candidate who begins to make preparations as to what he will do when in office, when the twelfth stage of Satyagraha

---

17   Shridharani, op. cit., p.33.
18   Ibid., p. 300.

is reached important governmental functions slowly are usurped. Specific, inert state activities again are made at least partially operative.

The culmination of Satyagraha comes in the formation of a parallel government to replace the existing order. To date, no Satyagraha ever has reached this plateau.

In the absence of relief from constitutional and legal recourse, the African American accepted the philosophy and made use of many of the facets of the previously described weapon of nonviolent direct action. By bringing the fighting into the open, the African American forced his oppressor to commit his acts of hostility where everyone could see him. In order to create an *anguished awareness* on the part of the nation, the African American was willing to subject himself to physical beatings, harassment, and even death if the occasion demanded it. The use of nonviolent action to supplement the process of change via jurisprudence indicates a growing sophistication and sense of involvement on the part of the African American segment of our society. But why did the African American employ nonviolent resistance instead of physical force to right the abuses he has been confronted with over the years?

The first, and probably the most logical, reason is that the African American subculture is disarmed. Consequently, it would be impossible for them to organize an army and win. Moreover the entrenched groups in society have control of the agencies of physical force and have no logistical problems as far as arms and ammunition are concerned.

Also, it is ludicrous to fight on a level where you cannot compete. If the *man* has all the lethal weapons at his disposal and you have none, you must find some method of attack that neutralizes his advantages. Realizing that moral force had as much strength as physical force gave the African American community the weapon they were seeking. Nonviolent direct action enabled the African Americans to shift the grounds upon which the *unfinished revolution* was to take place. As a result, the latent power of *the terrible meek* began to manifest itself.

In order to be successful, a Satyagraha operation must be preceded by a period of indoctrination and organization. This all takes time. However, because the movement is committed to nonviolence, it will have more freedom and less interference in its initial stages of development than a movement based on the bellicose use of force. This freedom from incipient restraint, which allowed for indoctrination and mobilization of the African American masses, is still another reason for the utilization of the weapon of nonviolent direct action.

The drama involved in nonviolent resistance constitutes a fourth reason for its employment by the African American community. Many portions of the white community will not automatically accede to African American demands. They are prone to inflict injuries upon the nonviolent demonstrators and use violence to combat their activities. This has a twofold effect on the civil rights movement. First, instead of cowing the African American masses it actually whetted their appetite for nonviolence, because many wanted to feel that they were doing their part in contributing to the alleviation of man's inhumanity to man. Second, the *pastures of complacent indifference* were awakened, and many members of the white culture because concerned about the indignities their black brothers were confronted with daily. Subsequently, many of these people channeled their concern into a civil rights organization that was actively working to overcome the African American's second-class citizenship.

Ten percent of America's population is African American. As a result, the broadest possible support is necessary if sufficient strength is to be mustered to carry the cause forward. Satyagraha offers to men, women, children, and the disabled the opportunity to become involved as active participants. For example:

> ...in Birmingham, some of the most valued foot soldiers were youngsters ranging from elementary pupils to teenage high school and college students... The lame and the halt and the crippled could and did join up.[19]

Far from having even the remotest tinges of exclusiveness, the nonviolent army is open to any and all who want to join.

The final reason for the employment of nonviolence was its effect upon the powerful structures which it was attempting to alter. Might did not make right, and the national spotlight began to focus on those sections of the country using police state tactics to suppress the constitutional rights of its citizens. Because the African American refused to employ violence, his opponent was confronted with a new method of resistance heretofore unemployed in America. As a result, the power structure often acted in a manner that solved nothing and generated more trouble that aroused the ire of the public at large. Instead of adjusting the contending claims, violence only tries to destroy the opposition. Only now does it appear that those in

---

19   Martin Luther King, Jr., *Why We Can't Wait* (New York: Harper and Row, Incorporated, 1963), p.38.

authority are beginning to realize that the power of the spirit cannot always be conquered by the power of the sword.

The words of Gandhi seem most fitting to terminate our discussion of the philosophy of the *unfinished revolution* as implemented by CORE: "If it comes true, it may be through the African Americans that the unadulterated message of non-violence will be delivered to the world."[20]

Founding of the Los Angeles Chapter of CORE

The year 1943 saw the development of a CORE affiliate in Pasadena, California. However, due to the fact that this chapter was somewhat restricted by its geographical location, a Los Angeles group began to emerge. In 1946 this assemblage was officially organized as Los Angeles CORE. Earl Walter, a social worker, became chairman of the organization in 1951 and served in that capacity until 1963, when he became Chairman Emeritus.[21] Long before civil rights demonstrations were reported in the popular press, Earl Walter and his wife, and a small group of dedicated people, were busy testing discrimination in hotels and motels, and suing the proprietors in court.

Initially, nonviolent direct action was practiced in a rather sporadic fashion by the Los Angeles chapter. An interracial group sat-in at the downtown Los Angeles tearoom of Bullock's in 1947 when the restaurant refused to serve African Americans. This venture ended in success and facilitated mild growth of the chapter. Basically, however, the years from 1948 to 1960 were lean ones as membership never exceeded twenty-five persons, no office had been established, financial resources were low or nonexistent, and all operations were handled on a shoestring.

The increasingly effective utilization of the sit-ins as a tool of nonviolent action spurred the growth of a previously stagnant membership. CORE opened its first office in 1960 when it shared quarters with the Fellowship of Reconciliation on Melrose Avenue. In 1961 it moved into its present headquarters at 1115 Venice Boulevard. The freedom rides caught national attention and enhanced the growth of CORE membership ranks across the country. The Los Angeles chapter was no exception, and since then gains have been registered in the group's size and activities.

---

20   Gandhi, op. cit., p.116.
21   Earl Lloyd Walter died of cancer on June 11, 1965, at the age of fifty-one.

Goals

As pointed out in Chapter II, all social movements have an ultimate aim toward which they direct all their activities. CORE is no exception. The general goal of Los Angeles CORE "is the elimination of discrimination based on religion, race, skin color, or national origin in all phases at all levels of American life."[22]

CORE has a program aimed at elimination of specific areas of discrimination and intolerance in Los Angeles that includes the following goals:

Employment: That each person should be hired on the basis of what he can do, not on the basis of his skin color.

Housing: That each family be allowed to live in any home it can afford, regardless of color.

Education: That all children be given equal educational opportunities.

Police
Malpractices: To guarantee that each person has full protection by the police.

Legislative
Action: Equal protection under the law.

Bail Fund: To establish a fund to cover this enormous but indispensable expense.

Chapter Housing
& Equipment: To be able to afford housing adequate for our needs.

Direct Action: To confront those who discriminate and to publicize acts of discrimination with more and more direct actions: sit-ins, picket lines, etc.

The CORE
Staff: Two full-time office people. A full-time printer. A field representative to investigate complaints and publicize CORE.

Financing: Never to let any CORE project fail due to lack of funds, and to finance more and more projects.[23]

---

22 CORE, *Constitution of the Los Angeles Congress of Racial Equality* (Los Angeles: CORE, 1963), p.1. (Mimeographed).

23 CORE, *Our Proposal to Make a Dream Come True* (Los Angeles: CORE, 1964), pp.6-18.

These goals represent an ambitious program that must involve the efforts of hundreds of people and thousands of dollars if they are to be realized. In the past CORE has done much to erase the color line in Los Angeles: yet, it is obvious that there is much more to do.

Government and Organization of Los Angeles CORE

In order to understand how any operating unit functions, every observer should make at least a rudimentary analysis of its government and structure. It is with a view toward this objective that this section is presented. A schematic diagram of the organization of CORE is shown in Figure 2.

CORE is essentially a membership rather than a leadership organization. "The top leaders can never depart far from the thinking of the rank and file without being made aware of it."[24] CORE's philosophy implies that, in fact, each chapter is an *action committee* in its entirety. The organization operates as a sort of *committee of the whole*. The passage of time, however, has seen the development of a more formal structure as the group has become more institutionalized. Even though there is a visible line of demarcation between the active membership and the executive committee, a very informal, flexible, and fluid operating procedure is very evident.

---

24 Lipset, op. cit. p.211.

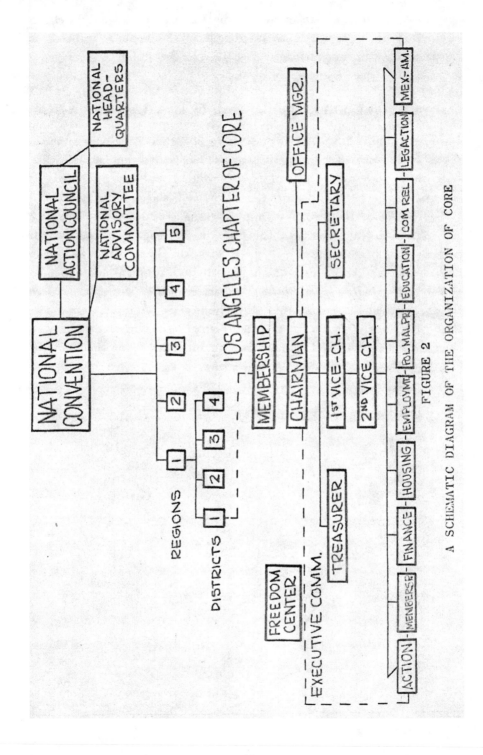

A SCHEMATIC DIAGRAM OF THE ORGANIZATION OF CORE

FIGURE 2

44

Because CORE is a grass-roots, democratic body, sovereign authority lies with the active membership. During at least two regularly scheduled general membership meetings per month all proposed CORE direct actions and most other activities of importance must be passed upon with majority approval. It would appear, then, that the active membership holds a rather tight grip on the functions the organization performs. In actuality this is not always true, for two reasons. First, membership meetings sometimes are very poorly attended. This enables a group within CORE desiring a particular proposal to mobilize its forces and receive a favorable vote with little opposition. Secondly, and more importantly, there is a feeling in the organization that the whole show is being run by an *in crowd*, the executive committee (five officers plus the chairmen of the standing committees). Due to the fact that there has been a lack of communication between the executive body and the general membership, most adherents feel that the executive committee is out of touch with reality and is really "trying to hold the movement back." They feel that the work of the organization should be thrown back into the hands of perhaps a small, but certainly tightly knit and extremely active general membership. In order to accomplish this, the more active members are now attempting to have a new constitution adopted that would, among other things, place committee chairmanships and projects directorships on a competitive basis. In the final analysis, however, CORE remains primarily a membership organization.

Currently, CORE utilizes the line and staff concept of organization and administration. The chairman of CORE is the chief overseer of the chapter. He also is responsible for staffing all the permanent and temporary committees upon recommendation of the committees. These appointments are ratified by the membership within thirty days. As the group's highest elected official, he sets the agenda and presides at general membership meetings and meetings of the executive committee. He also has the responsibility of representing the organization at all major functions and meetings. Finally, he deals with the larger community by talking with politicians in an attempt to get them to pass favorable civil rights legislation, by taking speaking engagements to project the dynamics and goals of CORE, and by entering into sessions of negotiations with business firms to bring about desired changes in employment practices.

At the moment Don Smith holds the number one position in CORE. Born in the Virgin Islands, he received a degree at the University of Puerto Rico. He makes his living as a freelance public relations agent. Although a member of CORE for sixteen years, he earned his leadership position the hard way. He has been arrested a number of times for civil rights activities and has served in almost every phase of the chapter's operations. Normally, he puts in an eight or nine hour day, seven days a week. In addition, his income has dropped considerably as a result of his prominent involvement in the civil rights movement. (CORE pays him no salary; he receives only a very small expense account.) The following interview gives a graphic portrait of CORE, its leader, and the civil rights movement in general.

Bartling: Why did you join CORE?
Smith: I felt it was the most significant way of expressing my desire to overcome segregation and discrimination in our society. Before moving over to CORE, I was a member of the Urban League and the NAACP.
Bartling: What do you foresee as the future of the civil rights movement?
Smith: It is not as limited today as formerly. It is broader in scope. I think it will take on newer and wider aspects, that is, political aspects. There will be an increase in political action. CORE and SNCC are responsible for the Mississippi Freedom Party. In 1964, for the first time, the national convention permitted CORE chapters to back candidates for office. Plans are also under way to establish a lobbyist in Washington to propose and oppose legislation. The area of employment also has changed. Formerly, if they discriminated, you would go into direct action. Now employers sign pledges that they will not discriminate and then do not perform. So we must continue to perform.
Bartling: What do you foresee as the future of Los Angeles CORE?
Smith: Basically, we need a greater relation with the minority community. In order to enlist their support, we have to concentrate on projects that will assist them. The minority community must trust and have faith in our organization. Operation Jericho is a good example of what I mean. Here workers went block to block, house to house. A block leader emerged around whom people could unite to solve their problems. After one block is organized you go on to the next. Eventually, community organization is developed by a steam roller effect. This strategy was employed in Watts to fight Proposition 14.
Bartling: How successful has Los Angeles CORE been?

Smith: We have been moderately successful, about the same as in other cities. Employment is a good example. A number of establishments abolished their discriminatory hiring and promotion practices after being confronted with our demands. CORE is now invited to participate in many community projects. Take the War on Poverty, for example. CORE is part of the planning body to set up a federation of groups to act as an umbrella agency to administer the program.

Bartling: Are there any concluding remarks you would like to make?

Smith: Yes. I should like to emphasize the fact that there are many groups working in the field of civil rights because there is more than one approach to the problem. Fragmentation has taken place because of a difference in opinion on how militant an organization should be. However, in Los Angeles this has been less noticeable than in other areas. We have only six active groups—CORE, UCRC, NVAC, Urban League, NAACP, and WCLC—fighting discrimination, whereas New York has about 150 and Chicago has approximately 100.[25]

The first and second vice chairmen assume the duties of the chairman in the event of his absence or unavailability. They coordinate all committee efforts and work within the organization as *inside men*, whereas the chairman does a great deal of outside work in the community. At the moment the first vice chairman has not indicated whether or not he is going to remain on the job; he is presently inactive. The second vice chairman has resigned to go to Europe.

The secretary and the treasurer have the usual responsibilities assigned to these roles. However, the secretary has taken a leave of absence to tour the South and the treasurer has resigned, further complicating CORE's financial position. The vacancy of four out of five of CORE's elective offices lends credence to the fact that this is, indeed, a membership organization.

CORE's only salaried employee is Walter Gilbert, the organization's full-time office manager. A high school dropout at seventeen, he joined CORE because he "was born Jewish in a right wing area and was spit on when little." Consequently, he "felt a certain amount of empathy with the Negro." A typical day finds Gilbert answering the telephone, taking care of correspondence, mimeographing and folding special mailings, and

25   Personal interview, June 23, 1965.

supervising whatever other office activities are currently in progress. For working nine to twelve hours a day, six days a week, he receives Forty-five dollars per week. Gilbert's commitment to the African American movement is total. He has stated that five years from today, somewhere, someplace, the cause will still have the benefits of his services.

The chapter's executive committee, which is comprised of the organization's five officers and the chairmen of its nine standing committees (the organizational chart, Figure 2, page 84, shows ten standing committees, but the Mexican-American committee has ceased to exist), furnishes most of the group's leadership and direction. CORE's Constitution outlines the following duties of the executive committee:

1.   …discusses plans and policies for the organization,
2.   brings recommendations to the membership based on reports from the committees,
3.   makes decisions on matters referred to it by the membership,
4.   and is empowered to make decisions of an emergency nature which cannot be delayed until a membership meeting[26]

In order to carry out any or all of these duties, a quorum of at least nine is necessary. Moreover, every decision the executive committee makes is subject to a veto by the active membership.

According to CORE's Constitution, the group has ten standing committees. However, further investigation reveals that only seven meet with some degree of regularity, two meet very infrequently, and one has now been abolished. Theoretically, the membership committee serves as CORE's socialization agent. It is responsible for developing and guiding the newly affiliated adherent in such a way that he will not only meet, but will surpass all membership requirements. It fulfills this obligation by sponsoring two orientation sessions and a nonviolent direct action workshop for all new members. In addition, it is supposed to keep membership records, collect dues, plan programs for recruiting new members, and regularly make personnel audits to ascertain whether or not members are meeting the obligations of active membership. The downward path of membership attests to how poorly the functions of this committee are being carried out.

The finance committee is in charge of revenues and expenditures.[27] It carries on fund raising projects to generate income for the chapter, and it

26   CORE, *Constitution…*, op. cit., Section I, Article 4.
27   A more penetrating analysis concerning finances will be made in a later

authorizes the payment of ordinary operating expenses.[28] Eva Newton, a thirty-four year old African American office machine operator, is currently the chairman of this committee. She was given the job one and a half months ago (May, 1965) and this probably accounts for the fact that she has had no financial training or fund raising experience whatsoever. Miss Newton feels the primary task of her committee is to choose the most pressing bill among the chapters many debts and discharge it. Once again the observer gets some indication of the internal weaknesses of CORE. Its financial position is further complicated by the fact that the finance committee has never prepared a budget, balance sheet, or income statement. At the moment CORE is in what might be called *financial receivership*. All records and financial documents have been turned over to a Certified Publish Accountant in the hope that he can untangle the maze and put the books back in order.

The housing committee, the employment committee, the police malpractices committee, and the education committee all investigate conditions of discrimination in their particular areas of endeavor and then recommend action to eliminate such treatment. For example, the police malpractices committee is constantly looking into charges of police brutality and has consistently recommended the establishment of a civilian police review board to alleviate unfair police treatment. Committee members feel that such a board would cause the police to discipline themselves better. Moreover, they think it would restore the faith of minority groups in the police because it would analyze civilian complaints against the police and suggest remedies and punishments to police commissioners. The outcome, CORE believes, would be an "improved climate of community trust." As yet, this goal is unrealized.

The legislative action committee attempts to bring about the enactment of pertinent legislation relating to civil rights, while at the same time urging the implementation of existing laws. CORE's community relations committee carries on the type of activity that seeks to involve previously uncommitted people and thus give *muscle* to the position taken by the organization on various matters. Speakers' bureaus, classes, and discussion groups are employed to increase citizen involvement. This committee serves as CORE's liaison with other community and civil rights organizations. Finally, as CORE's press agent, it is responsible for all communications to mass media.

---

section.
28 Other expenditures are authorized by vote of the membership.

Remembering that CORE is organized around action, it is easy to understand the significance of the action committee. A demonstration does not just happen spontaneously. In each instance a carefully followed procedure is used before employing direct action or civil disobedience. Initially, some member of the community may file a complaint alleging discrimination and/or one of the chapter's committees may turn up evidence of discrimination after appropriate investigation. The committee handing the complaint, after gathering sufficient data with which to construct a sound case, attempts to enter into negotiations with the discriminating party. If the party breaks down, the committee may vote on a recommendation for direct action, being aware of such factors as the necessity of mobilizing as much community support as possible before entering into any action, the forces at the organization's disposal, and the man hours and money necessary to achieve the desired goal. CORE never likes to enter into an action where the chances of success are nonexistent because any victory, no matter how small, helps them grow. If the committee passes on the recommendation, its chairman makes a report to the executive committee. After hearing the report, a majority of the executive committee makes a positive or negative recommendation to the general membership during one of its regularly scheduled meetings. The membership must approve the action by a two-thirds vote before it can be sent to the action committee for implementation. Working with the originating committee and the negotiating team, it organizes and carries through the desired plans. It has responsibility for complementing all arrangements for an action and for mobilizing all necessary participants.

The twenty-four-year-old chairman of the action committee, Cleveland Wallace, has been arrested three times for civil rights demonstrations. He joined CORE because he "felt the need for action." He considers the goal of his committee to be "how much we can get done." According to Wallace, "The job is what counts, not the person holding the job. Victory is measured in terms of the successes CORE puts over." A schematic diagram on the organization of the direct action committee is presented in Figure 3.

CORE has been and is now experiencing the burden of a constitution which provides for numerous *standing* and *sub* committees for which there are not enough people to make a quorum. In addition, the organization often has operated for considerable time periods without chairman for some of the important standing committees. All this is indicative of the fact that CORE's committee structure needs significant alteration.

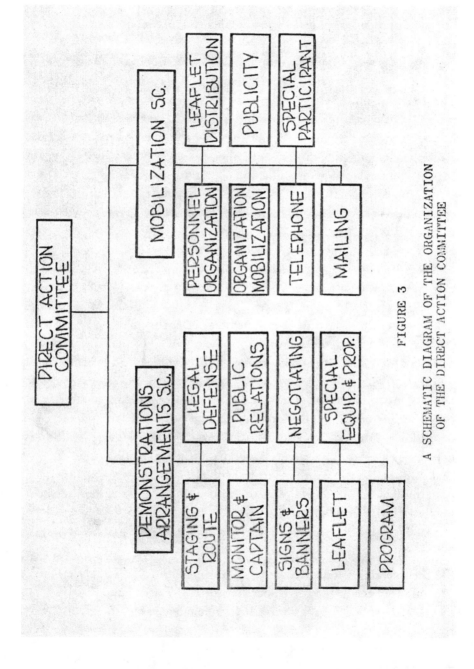

FIGURE 3

A SCHEMATIC DIAGRAM OF THE ORGANIZATION
OF THE DIRECT ACTION COMMITTEE

In an attempt to do something about this situation, the chapter currently is considering a proposal that would abolish all permanent committees except finance, membership, and   community relations. *Project directors* would be established in the areas of employment, police malpractice, housing, legislative action, and education.

Instead of working with a standing committee, the project directors would assign cases in their particular field to people in the general membership body. The general membership would operate as the action committee, with the project directors functioning as leaders of specific actions. As it stands now, having an action committee within a direct action organization signifies the creation of an entity within an entity because CORE's philosophy implies that, in fact, each chapter is an "action committee" in its entirety.

Right now, chairmen of standing committees are appointed by the chairman upon recommendation of the committees. If the new proposal is adopted, all committee chairmen and project directors would be elected by the general membership, thereby avoiding any political *spoils system* and creating competition among members who desire a chairmanship in a particular area.

Although the Freedom Center is sponsored by CORE and is using its name, the people who run it, and not the CORE membership, control it. Alice Trivedi, a former social worker for the city of Los Angeles, contributed five hundred dollars of her own money for development of the center and is presently its executive director. A very new institution, the Freedom Center held its first function on June 25, 1965. It was a meeting to discuss the programs and projects of the center. Located at 10203 ½ Compton Avenue, it will furnish tutorial service, African American history classes, educational trips for children, and social services of many kinds for adults. CORE hopes that projects like the Freedom Center will improve the organization's image in both the black and the white communities, and will generate new members for the chapter's undermanned ranks.

Meetings

On the second and fourth Thursdays of each month CORE holds its regular general membership meetings. Because the meetings are closed, only active members, members on approval, associate members, and individuals invited by a member have the right to attend. All sessions are conducted under the procedure outlined in *Robert's Rules of Order.*[29]

---

29   The observations to follow are based on the general membership meeting held

CORE's monthly bulletin states that the general membership meeting will convene at 8:00 PM; it seldom gets under way before 8:45 or 9:00 PM.[30] CORE places little premium on conforming the established schedules. The meeting hall at 4016 South Central Avenue is very bland and the only symbolism present is the American flag.

On February 18, 1965 the meeting was called to order and the minutes were read. Then, instead of immediately hearing committee reports, candidates for City Councilman from the Ninth District presented their credentials. CORE members quizzed the office seekers on everything from Proposition 14 to police review boards. Although Los Angeles CORE never officially backs an individual, just an *issue*, it was apparent that many of the members were less than satisfied with Gilbert Lindsey's (the incumbent) record.

Various committee reports were heard, and the membership book was passed around. This is a unique device by which CORE keeps track of those individuals who regularly participate, and thus are eligible to vote.

Next in order is old and new business. It is at this stage that rank and file members contribute their points of view, and it is here that *cleavages* can split the organization. There is an ever present dichotomy between the *more* militant faction and the *less* militant faction. Significantly, the bulk of CORE members are on one side or the other; therefore, the opportunity for compromise rarely presents itself. Moreover, this division cuts across ethnic lines, as black and white members are found together in both camps. Inability to reach a consensus on basic philosophy has seriously impaired CORE's effectiveness. When the *more* militant faction was defeated in their attempt to elect their choice for chairman in November 1963, they severed their ties with CORE and established the Nonviolent Action Committee (NVAC). CORE cannot stand such fragmentation, especially when those forming the splinter groups have been among the most active in the chapter. Moreover, the cleavage remains. Apparently, the split had no effect because a broad meeting of the minds has yet to be achieved.

Although precise statistics are not available, CORE's total membership is approximately 300 to 400, while active membership never exceeds 100. Forty-five members were present at the February 18 meeting, indicating a lack of *sense of involvement* on the part of most members, and the ability of one faction, if it so desired, to push through motions favorable to its point of

---

February 18, 1965; however, the general pattern of events was observed in subsequent meetings.

30 The same situation was noted when analyzing the committee meetings.

view. In addition, the meetings are so long in duration, members often vote on the basis of *the lateness of the hour* rather than on the soundness of the proposal under discussion.

Normally the executive committee initiates discussion on various proposals and recommends to the membership body what it feels would be in the best interests of the organization. The strength and enthusiasm of the membership determines whether or not the executive committee's view will prevail.

Leadership in the meeting depends on the political and social needs of the time. One month politics may be important, hence the legislative action chairman reigns supreme. Six months later, however, housing may take on special significance. It is imperative to remember that CORE is moved by the prevailing situation in the community. As a result, it is always changing. This has an effect on group dynamics. In CORE all power and authority do not necessarily rest with the personnel represented on the group's organizational chart. It is vested in many members holding no elected offices.

After all old and new business is taken care of, the meeting is adjourned. It is important to bear in mind that these gatherings are working meetings, and not for show. CORE is an effective group, but one would never know it by observing a meeting.

Hoping to make meetings more successful, some CORE members have proposed that the general membership meet weekly instead of bimonthly. They feel that this would throw the work of the organization back into the laps of a small, but nevertheless tightly knit and extremely active body. In addition, they feel that the project directors and committee chairmen should distribute mimeographed sheets of what has been transpiring in their particular areas of concern. In this way a great deal of time now spent on petty floor discussions would be saved, thereby making meetings shorter and more effective.

Membership Recruitment and Socialization

Membership in Los Angeles CORE is divided into two categories: active and associate.[31] An associate member is really adherent in name only because he does not participate in any of CORE's projects, even though he makes monetary contributions and desires to be informed of the group's activities.[32] An associate member may attend meetings, but he many not vote or hold office.

---

31   Contributing, supporting, sustaining, and lifetime members are just more expensive types of associate membership status.
32   As a participant observer, the writer held associate member status.

Active members are supposed to participate in the chapter's action projects on a regular basis, attend general membership meetings, and serve on one or more of the standing committees. Active members can vote and may hold office.

The procedure for admission as an active member is relatively simple. By filling out an application and paying one year's dues, an individual becomes a *member on approval*. A member on approval engages in the same activities as an active member, but during this period he cannot vote or hold office. CORE feels that each new recruit should demonstrate his commitment to the employment of nonviolent direct action before he has a vote as well as a voice in making decisions as to how to go about it. During this probationary period the new member is required to attend three orientation meetings to better equip him to fulfill his obligations as a member of the chapter. Orientation one deals with CORE's background and general perspective, two concerns the organization's structure, and three is a training session in the techniques of nonviolent direct action.

After approximately three months, if the new member has fulfilled the necessary requirements, upon recommendation of the membership committee and a majority vote of the general membership, the member on approval achieves active status.

At the present time the orientation sessions lack continuity because they are given on different days during different weeks. If they were held once a month for a two-day period they would be better coordinated and more meaningful, and would develop a better educated membership body.

CORE has a problem with determining what members should have the right to vote. Technically, the membership committee should analyze their files every three months to determine those eligible for voting. However, they are not performing this function. As a result, non-participants often set policy, even though they contribute little or nothing to the organization. In order to eliminate this situation the group advocating a new constitution has proposed that all project directors and committee chairmen keep accurate lists of individuals working actively in their spheres of concern. These lists would then be presented at the first meeting of every month, and the names appearing on them would be the voters for that month. It seems totally incongruous with the principles of CORE that someone who will not or cannot participate in the chapter's activities should be able to dictate acceptance or rejection of an action or how it is to be carried out.

The obvious question now arises: what type of individual joins CORE and commits himself to the principles of nonviolent direct action and why?

While generalizations are dangerous and often meaningless, it is possible to present some broad hypotheses about the organization's adherents.

1. Membership composition is interracial: Caucasians, Mongolians, and Blacks are all present in varying degrees.
2. The majority of members are from the lower social economic stratum in our society.
3. A low level of education attainment is present among most members.
4. Without exception, CORE members are affiliated with the Democratic Party.
5. The membership as a whole is on the young side.
6. Some members join in the hope of achieving political goals.
7. Some whites join for paternalistic reasons.
8. Members may join because of their own frustrations and problems.
9. Some individuals like the publicity and the excitement of demonstrations.
10. Individuals sincerely dedicated to fighting discrimination in all its sundry forms are found in abundance.
11. Many African Americans join because "they were born black."[33]

While many of the above statements speak for themselves, a few need elaboration. That many of the members are from the lower socio-economic group is attested to by their occupational position. When asked, "How do you make a living?" the most frequent reply was "At the moment I am at large." Moreover, those who do work seldom have the prestige of a white-collar job or a position that will allow them to become independently wealthy.

Currently, the bulk of CORE members are affiliated with the Democratic Party because they feel that it is the political organization most responsive to their appeals. It is interesting to note, however, that this support really is functional, because a number of interviews revealed that the same members who backed Lyndon Johnson in 1964 would support a Republican in 1968 if they felt he would advance the African American cause.

Even rudimentary analysis reveals the fact that most of CORE's members are under thirty years of age. The office manager is seventeen, the former treasurer was twenty-four, the action committee chairman is twenty-four,

---

33 Many people feel that individuals join CORE because of a desire for personal gain. They feel that these people are using the African American cause for their own benefit. Although this many be the case, this observer found no evidence of it.

and the Freedom Center manager is eighteen, to cite just a few examples. This dedicated body of adherents, while low on experience, which is not hurting the organization, brings to CORE a tenacious enthusiasm that should allow the chapter to prosper in years to come. They lend credence to Eric Hoffer's contention "that we hardly know how things happened in history unless we keep in mind that much of the time it was juveniles who made them happen."[34]

Some members join in the hope of achieving desired political goals. While these individuals are a very small minority, they are nevertheless present. For example, a socialist who thinks that there should be a redistribution of income adheres to CORE's principles because he thinks his program has a better chance of being realized here than anywhere else. Mary Humphrey, a twenty-year old CORE member for two years, is a pacifist and feels that "discrimination is not really the problem."

Again in the minority, but still present, are those people who join CORE for paternalistic reasons. These are the white people who see themselves as the "savior of the downtrodden black man." They feel that only through their efforts will the African American be returned to his rightful place in society.

CORE has members who joined because of frustrations and problems in their personal lives. By being involved in the civil rights movement they find a new identity and a new outlet for their pent-up emotions. This fact is visually demonstrated by the amount of miscegenation and cohabitation present among CORE members. Some of the white women, unable to compete successfully for a man in their own society, now achieve a sense of personal satisfaction by developing a *meaningful* social relationship with an African American in the chapter.

Many members, especially the younger ones, enlist in CORE's ranks because they like the publicity and excitement of demonstrations. These followers are contributing to CORE's membership problems because they do not understand that membership entails responsibility. They join, but in a few months they fall away because they really do not want to get involved in the day-to-day routine work.

The antithesis of the aforementioned type of member is the person who is sincerely dedicated to fighting racial injustice. Although the total active membership is small, these persons constitute the majority of that body. These are people like Michael Hannon, "a seven-year veteran policeman, a family man with four kids, a bright, articulate young man of 28 trying to

---

34   Eric Hoffer, "A Time of Juveniles," *Harper's*, CCXXX (June, 1965), 16.

better himself by studying law at night, "[35] who feel that a man should be judged by the color of his character, not the color of his skin. Due to his active participation in the civil rights movement, he has been temporarily suspended from the police force.

The most often used answer by African Americans to the question concerning membership was "I was born black" or "Being an African American started me in the movement." Robert Bailey, a forty-seven year old retired engineer, falls into this category. In addition to his membership in CORE he is also the Southern California district chairman for CORE. He devotes full time to the movement and serves without pay as district chairman. He feels that "discrimination is woven into the fabric of our society because once a minority becomes assimilated in our country, it begins to discriminate itself." Consequently, his goal is to "change society into a state of mutuality."

At the moment CORE's active membership is small because the organization appears to have no specific focal point. It needs to get an issue or an idea that people can associate with. Police brutality might mobilize the African American masses in Los Angeles if it is handled in the right way. The chapter is plagued by a large turnover in both membership and leadership. For example, in the last eight months CORE has had three office managers. Moreover, it appears that many of the members are afraid of doing any very hard work. A member will participate in a demonstration and that will be the extent of his involvement. Many members seem to forget about the hours of investigation and negotiation that precede an action and the follow-up efforts to make sure that the *wrong* has been corrected. There can be no progress, no achievement, without sacrifice; therefore, even though it takes a certain type of person to join and work, it many not be amiss to suggest that CORE set up a recruitment program to expand its following and reevaluate its inadequate orientation program.

Finances of Los Angeles CORE

CORE's financial position can be summed up in the poignant words of one of its most dedicated followers: "Money does not really matter." Although CORE is an organization that handles a great deal of money, it fails to recognize the importance of sound financial policies and practices. The recent turning over of whatever records existed to a certified public accountant indicates the extent of the chapter's financial chaos.

---

35 "Civil Rights: Odd Cop Out," *Newsweek*, LXV (June 21, 1965), 30.

A typical month's expenditures can only be an estimate of cash disbursements because the chapter keeps no balance sheet or income statement and the treasurer's records are inaccurate. The following expenses are those normally incurred by CORE in a typical month of operation:

Rent for office	$75
Rent for meeting hall	15
Office manager salary	180
Chairman's expense account	48
Telephone	500
Mailings	100
Office supplies	50
Electricity	<u>20</u>
	$988

Most of the above expenses are fixed costs; that is, they continue as long as the organization remains in existence. However, some of the variable costs, like the expensive telephone bill, can be controlled, and it is here that CORE should initiate some cost cutting procedures immediately.

It should be pointed out here that CORE's official labor costs only $228 per month. If it were not for the immeasurable hours of volunteer labor donated by many members, this expense would soar. Moreover, these same people often incur expenses in carrying out the chapter's work for which they are not compensated.

One significant item has thus far been omitted from CORE's expense statement. This is the sum the chapter must pay for bail bonds when a number of its members are arrested for demonstrating. In 1963 the chapter was almost bankrupted when it had to lay out ten thousand dollars in bail bond fees for the 249 persons arrested at Southwood. Again, in 1965, when civil rights demonstrators were arrested at the Federal Building, CORE spearheaded a drive to raise ten to fifteen thousand dollars to pay the premiums on eighty to one hundred thousand dollars in bonds. Even though the bail was reduced in many cases and donations had been received, this type of activity has left CORE with a considerable debt.

Bail bondsmanship is one of the most vital services the militant African American uses today because it is an absolute necessity for people who get into trouble with the law and find themselves in jail. Upon arrest a person is booked and fingerprinted. Then he has the opportunity to make a telephone call. Seeking his release on bail, Celes King III, CORE's bond specialist, is called. He goes to the jail, obtains the pertinent information he needs, signs the necessary bail papers, and the prisoner is released. For providing his service, King receives 10 per cent of the bail. It is obvious that if CORE had sufficient cash it could save a tremendous amount of money now spent for bond fees.

Besides being in business to make a profit, Celes King is in business to help people. It was King and his associates who arranged for the release from jail of more than 200 CORE demonstrators at a housing site in Torrance, California. Even though many of those arrested were out of state people and kids without adequate funds, he and his agency provided upwards of a hundred thousand dollars in bail bonds. If these people had *skipped out* on him, chances are his business would have been destroyed. Robert Hall, a former CORE member and now one of the leaders of NVAC, explained King's significance when he said, "Without him, there would be no militant civil rights movement in Los Angeles." There is no question about the fact that this African American bail bondsman, unsung hero though he has been, has provided valuable services to the African American's fight for equality.

The money for the aforementioned expenses has to come from somewhere. CORE relies primarily on membership dues, sale of civil rights material, contributions, and fund raising activities.

Remembering that there are only 300 to 400 people in CORE, membership dues cannot constitute a major source of revenue. Assuming 100 pay active fees of three dollars per year and 200 pay associate fees at five dollars per year, this would only bring in thirteen hundred dollars. The sale of civil rights bumper stickers and buttons adds a little to CORE's treasury. Periodic donations enhance CORE's bank balance. Probably the most important source of revenue for CORE is its fund raising activities. These take many forms: dance and /or dinner parties, a lecture or series of lectures, and entertainment benefits. On March 27, 1965 CORE had a dinner party (donation five dollars). After the dinner there was a dance (donation a dollar fifty). On April 28 they had a theater party at the Warner Playhouse where members were invited to attend the performance of two controversial plays: *Dutchman* and *The Toilet*. On June 4 a CORE A-GO GO at the Dooto Music Center was held to defray bail expenses for the Federal Building sit-ins. While many of these fund raising activities have been successful, some have not, and several people feel that they are not run properly. Many have said the quality of entertainment has been weak, while others feel that no complimentary tickets should be given to CORE members, as is now the practice.

One of the most unique findings in this study was the fact that the amount of money CORE takes in depends, to a large extent, on the *situation*. If there is a Birmingham bomb blast of African American children, or a murder of CORE field workers, or a Selma march for justice, the money pours in because the population is aroused and concerned. However, if no such events occur, then the populous apparently assumes that all is well, and CORE's revenue sources dry up overnight. Many people in the Los Angeles area suffer from what is known as *thousand-mile-itis*. They feel that there are no problems in Los Angeles and send their money, instead, to Selma. Needless to say, this also impairs CORE's attempts to solicit funds.

In an attempt to smooth out the fluctuations in income, it might be wise if CORE hired a professional fund raiser. This suggestion has been presented in the past, but it has always been defeated because CORE members are very idealistic and do not want any outside interference. In addition, CORE might more actively recruit associate members who will contribute to the organization but not get involved in its functions. They should also attempt to solicit office supplies, such as paper, stamps, posters, and so on, from local merchants, in order to cut costs. Finally, they should more aggressively sell their civil rights stickers and buttons by sending teams to various gatherings where large groups of people will be present.

It is time for a new sophistication on the part of the membership as far as finances are concerned. No organization can continue indefinitely when its expenditures are forever exceeding its income.

CORE's Physical Plant

The condition of CORE's office at 1115 Venice Boulevard, Los Angeles, further reflects the poor fashion in which the organization is run. Although functional, it is in a continuous state of disorder. This can give some people a negative impression, and mirrors a certain amount of apathy on the part of the membership. A floor plan of the office layout is presented in Figure 4.

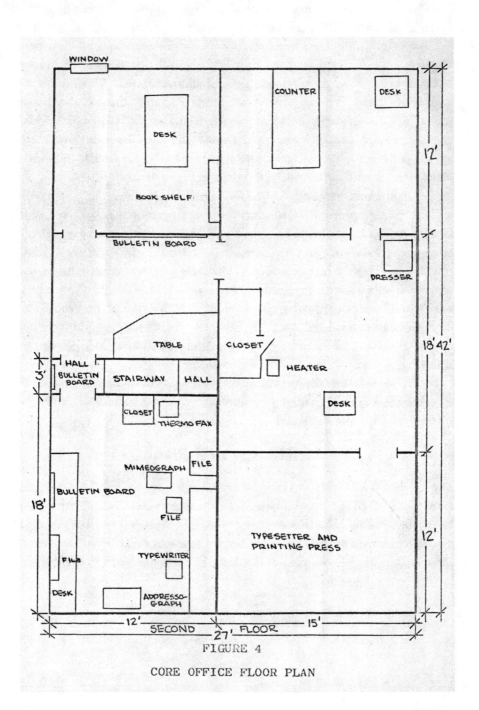

FIGURE 4

CORE OFFICE FLOOR PLAN

Following are some photographs of CORE's office which paint an accurate picture of the chapter's facilities and how they are maintained. Plate I shows the entrance to the office. The external condition of the building does not encourage any passerby to just walk in (in fact, it could be a definite impediment to such an act). Plate II shows the stairway leading to the second floor and the hub of all chapter activity. Plate III pictures the room where most of CORE's committees meet; it also serves as the chairman's office. Plate IV shows a collection of books, clothes, and other odds and ends that have been accumulating for a number of months on a table in the hallway. Apparently this area serves as a *giant receptacle*. This scene also indicates the general disorderliness of the office. Plates V and VI were taken in part of the office that often serves as a committee room when sufficient membership is present to justify using a larger area. In addition, demonstration signs and placards are stored here, and a printing press is housed in the front part of the room. The signs on the wall are typical of those one would expect to see in an organization like CORE. Plates VII and VIII picture the epicenter of the office. It is here that the office manager conducts the day-to-day affairs of the chapter. This is where mimeographed flyers are prepared for mailing. Files and equipment are stored here. Telephone calls requesting information on a variety of actions and activities are answered here, and this is the center of almost all of the chapter's informal "bull sessions" that often last until the early hours of the morning. Plate VII shows the office manager's desk, while Plate VIII catches Lou Smith, Western Regional Field Secretary for CORE, in an informal discussion.

At the moment most members appear to be unconcerned about their physical plant. However, a few of the more dedicated adherents have suggested that the responsibility for keeping the office and building clean rotate on a weekly basis between committee chairmen and project directors. (This is an excellent idea because right now no one is commissioned with janitorial responsibilities and the office reflects this most vividly).

PLATE I
Entrance to Core Office

PLATE II
Stairway to Second Floor

PLATE III
Corner of Committee Room

PLATE IV
Accumulated Articles

PLATE V
Demostration Signs in Larger Committee Room

PLATE VI
Desk in Larger Committee Room

PLATE VII
Office Manager's Desk

PLATE VIII
Lou Smith, Western Regional Field Secretary for Core

CORE's office is not located in an area where it can be immediately responsive to African American residents. The chapter is considering moving and situating their office somewhere in the heart of the *African American community* in order to expand their basis of support and concentrate on projects and services that will assist the African American in his daily life. A change of location, with an accompanying shift in emphasis, should assist CORE in establishing a needed *focal point* around which members can unite in building a stronger and more purposeful chapter.

CORE Symbolism

All organizations need some distinctive identifying features, and CORE is no exception. Although its recognition items are few, the chapter has its buttons, stickers, and martyrs. These symbols assist the individual in belonging to the group because they satisfy his inner self; they are a visible sign of something invisible (pride, uniqueness, and so on). Moreover, the CORE emblems aid, to some extent, in identifying and distinguishing CORE members from nonmembers of the group. Lastly, they create a great deal of interest, not only in their physical appearance but also as to what they represent.

CORE buttons (Figure 5) sell for twenty-five cents and carry such slogans as "Freedom Now" and "Let's End Discrimination." Their popularity is attested to by the number of chapter members who wear at least one almost all the time. CORE's "We Shall Overcome" bumper stickers cost fifty cents each and occupy the chrome on many a car in the Los Angeles area.

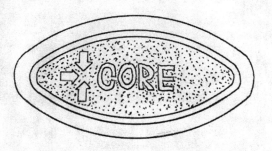

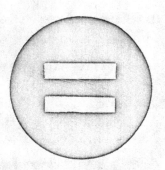

'We Shall Overcome'

FIGURE 5

CORE SYMBOLISM

69

A quotation on a CORE handout sheet indicates the importance of these symbols to the group's members:

> We array ourselves with buttons and pins and bumper stickers working for the day when they shall be cast out on yesterday's bleak landscape... but yesterday is today and the same old war horse still tramples human flesh... ands so we arm ourselves with buttons and pins and bumper stickers to identify ourselves with truth as that some day we sing about comes turning into now and all these trappings lie discarded on the junk pile of yesterday's bleak landscape.[36]

A number of individuals have sacrificed their lives for the civil rights movement. This list includes such people as:

Medgar W. Evers, 37, NAACP field secretary. Ambushed in Jackson, Miss., June 12, 1963.

Denise McNair, 11, Cynthia Wesley, Carol Robertson and Addie Mae Collins, 14, African American school girls. Killed in church bombing, Birmingham, Ala., September 15, 1963.

The Rev. James J. Reeb, 38, white Boston Unitarian minister, clubbed, Selma, Ala., March 9, 1965. Died, March 11.[37]

These martyrs symbolize a common ground around which the chapter unites because no members want the death of their comrades to be in vain.

CORE Publications

CORE publications fall into three categories: (1) the monthly calendar, (2) bulletins containing special announcements, and (3) political information sheets.

In order to keep the membership fully informed as to the chapter's activities, CORE publishes a monthly calendar that contains the name, place, and date of every function undertaken by the group. This is a very effective communication device and CORE has employed it well.

On a number of occasions situations have arisen after the monthly schedule has been prepared and posted; consequently, frequent bulletins containing information on specific subjects are mailed out. For example,

---

36   CORE, *Sales Bulletin on Buttons, Pins, and Stickers* (New York: CORE, n.d.).
37   Charles Morgan, Jr. "Southern Justice," *Look*, XXIX (June 29, 1965), 73.

during the Thriftimart demonstrations the action committee sent an emergency newsletter to all active CORE members and friends on the subject of *responsibility*, in the hope of attaining greater membership support so that the action could be intensified. Other announcements contain information on special meetings and fund raising benefits.

Periodically CORE publishes literature supporting particular issues and candidates. During the November 1964 election they sent out material attacking Proposition 14. In May 1965 CORE distributed political information sheets supporting Reverend James Jones during his campaign for office number two on the Los Angeles school board. The success of the communication media indicates that one should look elsewhere for the reason for the lack of response on the part of most CORE members.

Direct Action Tactics

Los Angeles CORE members have shopped in, picketed, boycotted, sat-in, and marched in an attempt to abolish racial discrimination in this area. They realize that aggressive behavior is most effective when it is well organized, adequately directed, and skillfully led. A number of "less than successful" actions have taught the chapter the value of organization.

Direct action tactics can be subdivided into three categories: demonstrations, non-cooperation, and intervention.[38] CORE employs the following forms of demonstrations: marches, picketing, and leaflet distribution. When Martin Luther King was arrested in Selma, Alabama, early in 1965 about 100 CORE members conducted a protest march through downtown Los Angeles. The march started at Olympic Boulevard and Broadway and terminated at the Spring Street entrance of the Federal Building. Marches presumably serve to dramatize an issue, educate the people as to what is transpiring in their environment, and mobilize public opinion in a favorable manner. It is doubtful that CORE marches have produced any of these objectives.

It is in the field of picketing that CORE has carried out some of its more *controversial* actions. On Monday, March 10, 1965, some twenty members

---

38 Martin Opppenheimer and George Lakey, *A Manual for Direct Action* (Chicago: Quadrangle Books, Incorporated , 1964), Chapter VII. Brewton Berry, *Race and Ethnic Relations* (Boston: Houghton Mifflin Company, 1958), Chapter V. Berry discussed several weapons organizations may use in their conflicts with others, among them being lynchings, race riots, pogroms, insurrections, strikes and boycotts, passive resistance, art, humor, litigation, and the ballot.

of CORE began protest picketing at the Federal Building in downtown Los Angeles. The action was scheduled to be carried on round the clock for three days, or until the planned protest march from Selma to Montgomery, Alabama, was successfully terminated. A picket line, similar to the one shown in Figure 6, was set up, and all participants were told to maintain discipline and to conduct themselves in a nonviolent fashion, regardless of what happened. Demonstrators were asked to observe the following rules:

(1)   The spokesman or picket captain is in complete charge; he is the only person to speak to bystanders. If anyone asks for information, refer him to the spokesman or picket captain.

(2)   It is most important that you do not respond to hecklers or speak to bystanders.

(3)   The spokesperson is the only person to speak to the press or public.

(4)   Do not show anger by look, speech, or manner.

(5)   Avoid excessive conversation within the group, and do nothing that would make the group seem disorderly. If there are Freedom Songs, the singing is to be unified and orderly.

(6)   If you have a question, direct it to the spokesman. For the duration of the action, his decisions are final.

(7)   If you wish to leave, speak to the spokesman.

(8)   In case of violence from others, you must, above all, remain calm and nonviolent. Do not raise your hands even to protect yourself. (You may cover your head, or in other ways protect your body, but do not give the appearance of striking back.) If a participant is injured, remain in your place. The spokesman or picket captain will assist the injured person. If the spokesman is injured, a previously assigned person will assist him and take over as spokesman, if necessary.

(9)   The sign should be held parallel to your body; keep it upright and avoid holding it sideways. Do not wave or shake it.

(10) Distance. Under normal circumstances two yards distance is enough space between pickets. This will allow a person to walk between you and not stop the line. Avoid walking too close to the next picket.[39]

---

39   CORE, *Instructions to Participants in Action Project* (Los Angeles: CORE, n.d.), p.1

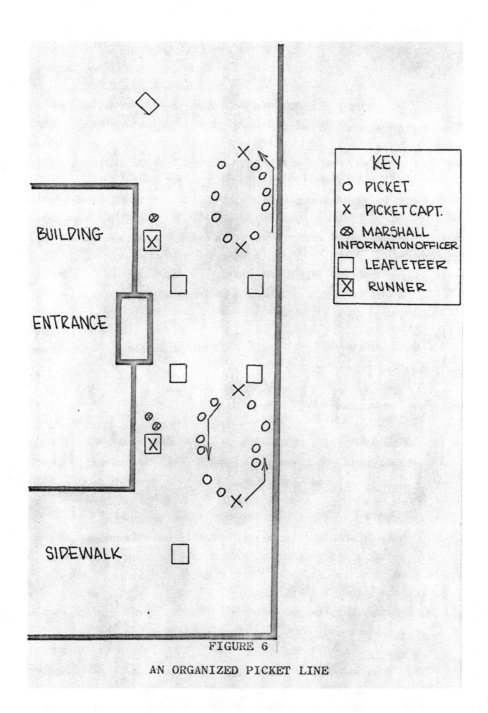

KEY

○ PICKET
✕ PICKET CAPT.
⊗ MARSHALL INFORMATION OFFICER
☐ LEAFLETEER
☒ RUNNER

BUILDING

ENTRANCE

SIDEWALK

FIGURE 6

AN ORGANIZED PICKET LINE

On Tuesday, CORE lost control of the demonstration when the protest moved into the building itself. About noon Ed Wilson, a field secretary for SNCC, told approximately 700 people outside the Federal Building that he was going to stage a protest rally in the office of the United States attorney on the sixth floor. He invited all those interested to join and follow him inside. Some forty persons answered the call. Filling the hallway to the attorney's office, they sang *We Shall Overcome*. They finally were persuaded to move, and they went to the lobby of the building and discussed whether or not they should vacate it. Again they were asked to leave, this time by the leaders of their own organization as well as by the United States attorney, who explained that the demands of the group were being forwarded to Washington. Ed Wilson, however, would have no part of this, and asked his followers to stay inside the building. "It's very nice that our demands are being forwarded."[40] At 5:30 pm the building closed and the demonstrators were removed by force because they refused to leave on their own accord. One example of the fact that CORE was no longer directing the action was pointed up by two participants who did not follow instructions and remain nonviolent. One was accused of biting the leg of a marshal, while another was accursed of jumping on the back of an officer and slugging him. Both were arrested.

Tuesday night about seventy-five demonstrators picketed the Federal Building. Wednesday morning found 150 demonstrators marching in the peaceful manner at the same site. However, the afternoon was a different story, and before the day was over ninety-eight were taken into custody. Twenty-nine persons were arrested for obstructing the movement of United States mail. A later sit-in demonstration resulted in more mass arrests. Over half of those arrested were high school and college students who were untrained in the techniques and methods of nonviolent direct action.

By Thursday activity was less turbulent. Forty pickets were present at the building. A federal court injunction now forbid demonstrations on the Federal Building property. Friday night twenty-three demonstrators began a pray-in on the steps of the Federal Building. "The group was led in prayers and civil rights hymns by the Rev. William Abbot, 36, a Presbyterian minister, and James Gallagher, 30, a graduate student at U.S.C."[41]

---

40   Walter Ames and Richard Main, "Rights Protest Causes Federal Building Melee," *The Los Angeles Times,* March 10,1965, p.27.

41   Robert Jackson, "All-Night Prayer Vigil Defies 8 L.A. Judges," *The Los Angeles Times,* March 13, 1965, p. 12.

On Saturday, March 13, the week's activities were climaxed with the largest racial demonstration in the history of Los Angeles. More than 6,000 men, women, and children marched from Pershing Square to the Federal Building to urge federal intervention in Selma, Alabama, and to honor the memory of Reverend James Reeb. The action was sponsored by several civil rights organizations in Los Angeles and the marchers were led by a number of civil rights leaders, including Don Smith of CORE.

Although a small group of pickets maintained a vigil outside the Federal Building during the week of March 14, to 20, for all intents and purposes the action begun by CORE on March 10,1965 was over. Only the aftermath remained. One hundred and one persons had been arrested, and money had to be raised for bail. CORE sponsored a *Bail Sunday* to raise money for the jailed demonstrators, but is still in debt as a result of this action. In addition, a number of people had to stand trial for their activities and could possibly draw jail terms and/or fines. More important, however, is the question of whether or not the action really accomplished anything. Because CORE initiated the first day's picketing, even though subsequent demonstrators broke out spontaneously, the chapter is at least partially responsible for the answer to this query. On the one hand we find those people who feel that the cause is impaired by violating the law. This point of view was expressed by the Reverend H. H. Brookins, Chairman of UCRC, when he said:

> We accept their motives but we differ with them on some of their tactics. Stopping the due process of federal officers here will not resolve the problem of lack of federal intervention in Selma.[42]

His views were echoed by the *Los Angeles Times,* in an editorial which stated that "no grievance justifies an unruly mob laying siege to a government building."[43]

The antithesis of the above was stated by Robert Hall, Chairman of NVAC, when he said that the action did not do any harm.

> What is harm? The Negro merchants down here on Central Avenue are doing harm because they are helping discrimination by not participating

---

42 Paul Weeks, "Tactics Used Here Dismay Rights Leaders," *The Los Angeles Times*, March 12, 1965, p.3.

43 "Times Editorials: Civil Rights and Wrong Protests," *The Los Angeles Times,* March 12, 1965, p. 4.

and by not putting money into the movement. As a matter of fact, I'm for more actions of this type.[44]

Hall's point of view was supported by James Garnett, head of SNCC in Los Angeles, who said: "no matter how many organizations get together, it's the people who are here and in jail who must decide as individuals on the propriety of their actions."[45]

In the final analysis, the answer to the success or failure of this action lies in the type of people who took part in the demonstration and the action's effect on public opinion. Youth was everywhere at the Federal Building.

"I would say 80% have been high school and college students who many have been active in organizations, but not in ours," said Cleveland Wallace, 24, Chairman of CORE's action committee.[46]

When Selma was gone, the kids were gone. This civil rights struggle is a long-term proposition which requires an organized following, not just *spur of the moment* adherents. Perspective and direction are needed because civil rights activities demand hard work.

This action did not disturb the conscience of Los Angeles whites. Its effect was just the opposite. It caused a great deal of animosity, and the reaction of many was, "Don't they have anything better to do than sit-in?" Or, in the words of *The Los Angeles Times*: "Through misguided zeal of mere exhibitionism, the demonstrators who flouted the law have demonstrated how not to gain sympathy and support."[47]

This action did succeed in focusing national publicity on the civil rights movement in Los Angeles and getting people on the picket line who CORE could not reach before. However, this really does not compensate for all the liabilities CORE incurred in the action. In the future they should make sure that all members are trained in the techniques of nonviolence before trying to engage in an action, that each participant rigidly adheres to the rules set up for the action, and that all organizations coordinate their efforts instead of working at cross purposes.

CORE has also been active in picketing different grocery store chains in an attempt to eliminate job bias in the retail food industry. Thiftimart Stores, Incorporated have been on the receiving end of most of this activity

---

44 Personal interview, June 23, 1965.
45 Weeks, loc. Cit.
46 Ibid., p. 35.
47 Ibid., p.4.

since April 1965 because they have steadfastly refused to negotiate equal job opportunities for minorities.[48]   In addition to the picketing, a number of *shop-ins* also were carried out against Thriftimart. The following instructions were given to participants in this demonstration:

(1) All demonstrators must have enough money on their persons to cover the total amount of prices on the items in their carts at all times.

(2) No demonstrator shall put pastries, ice cream, milk or other perishable goods in their carts.

(3) All demonstrators shall observe CORE rules for action...

(4) All demonstrators shall notify spokesman when coming or going.

(5) All demonstrators shall observe store displays and not knock them over.

(6) No arrests shall be included in this action.

(7) DO NOT SPEAK TO THE PRESS OR TO BYSTANDERS UNLESS YOU HAVE BEEN DESIGNATED AS A SPOKESMAN.[49]

Today, the finish to the Thriftimart story is yet to be written. The organization does have more African Americans working for it now than when direct action first was started. However, the action has been carried on sporadically for such a long period of time that member ship support for it has declined steadily. Moreover, this action has not generated any mass community involvement nor mobilized public opinion.

Direct action of the non-cooperation variety implies the withholding of cooperation with a foe. This technique may take several forms but CORE uses only one, the consumer's boycott, and they use it sparingly. During the Thriftimart action handbills were passed out urging people not to shop at Thriftimart and not to buy either Jerseymaid or Smart and Final products because Thriftimart owns 22.45 percent of Jerseymaid and eighty-four Smart and Final warehouses. The boycott was ineffective. The boycott did not solidify the minority groups, and many of them continued to patronized Thriftimart stores.

---

48 CORE has insisted that the Food Employers' Council, who represent Thriftimart, supply them with statistics on the company's racial employment breakdown. The Council has responded that any data they furnish must be on an industrywide basis. Hence the reason for CORE's direct action against Thriftimart.

49 CORE, *Instructions to Participants* .., p.2.

Intervention, the last of the three categories of direct action, embodies interference that may affect the interests of others. CORE makes use of such intervention tools as the sit-in, the fast, and the freedom rides. The chapter's latest sit-in was held at the office of Mayor Samuel Yorty to protest his opposition to the YOB-EOF merger. Inability to agree on the composition of a local antipoverty board was holding up federal funds for most new poverty projects, and CORE felt that the African American was suffering because of the delay. The action was carried to the home of the mayor where seven pickets, including Don Smith, marched for about one and a half hours. "Smith said the reason for picketing the mayor's home was to 'dramatize the situation for the public.'"[50] It is doubtful that this was accomplished.

In order to intensify the Thriftimart action, CORE began a hunger strike on May 20, 1965, at 12:00 noon. Louis Smith, one of the National CORE's field secretaries, began a fast that was to continue on a twenty-four hour basis until the management of Thriftimart agreed to negotiate with CORE to find ways to end their discriminatory practices. This action was not successful because of the reluctance of the chapter's executive board to participate. Membership response and support were almost nonexistent, and the event received little publicity.

CORE chartered a bus so that some of their members could participate in Dr. Martin Luther King's Selma to Montgomery march. The trip was really a reward for those people who engaged in the Federal Building picketing. The group of thirty-eight was interracial and young in composition, the average age being somewhere around twenty. The trip vividly showed each participant the problems that really exist in the South. Upon returning, many said: "You don't really know what it's like down there until you become a part of it for a few days." All agreed that the bus trip and march whetted their appetite for deeper involvement in the civil rights movement.

Overall, it seems that CORE's tactics have been both beneficial and detrimental. While they have achieved some notable victories, they have alienated public opinion on many occasions. There can be no doubt that there is a basis for protest in most of the actions they undertake. In the future CORE protests might meet with greater results if they were better

---

50   Paul Weeks, "Break Hinted in Poverty Dilemma; CORE Holds Yorty Office Sit-In," *The Los Angeles Times*, May 29, 1965, p. 13.

planned, organized, directed, and controlled, and if they did not trample the rights of others by violating the law.

The Years Ahead

CORE's future is far from assured. The chapter is confronted with a multitude of problems, such as:

1. A steadily declining membership;
2. An unrealistic constitution;
3. Cleavages among members as to degree of militancy;
4. A serious lack of funds with which to operate;
5. Weak internal organization that is impairing the chapter's effectiveness;
6. Lack of a focal point upon which to concentrate the energies of the organization;
7. A poor image in the African American community;
8. Apathetic response on the part of the membership for most chapter activities;
9. Selection of action projects that, for the most part, are ineffective.

Additional progress in the field of civil rights is going to be difficult, especially when such anti-African American organizations as the White Citizens Council and the John Birch Society are flourishing. Consequently, CORE must mobilize its forces and reorganize for greater strength on a broader scale.

CORE's future lies in the minority community. It should not shackle itself by becoming too involved in national problems; rather it should concentrate on situations at home. CORE should make greater efforts to create programs, activities, and services of a self-help nature that will meet the interests and needs of the minority community.[51]

The day of the demonstration is passing. Therefore, although CORE should use direct action tactics where appropriate, other methods should be pressed into service. The most potent of the new techniques is political power. The African American needs to be educated concerning politics in Los Angeles. CORE should now devote considerable time and energy to political education and voter registration. By building a "grass roots" organization in

---

51   CORE has made a start in this area by setting up a Freedom Center and by establishing a committee to look for new office space somewhere in the heart of the African American community.

the minority community, the chapter could exercise considerable power in the political arena and advance the cause of civil rights accordingly. Tomorrow, CORE's commitment must be to something greater than disturbing the peace if the African American's status in the Los Angeles area is to be improved.

CHAPTER IV

The Changing Nature
of the Civil Rights Movement

○ ○

If peaceful revolution is impossible,
then violent revolution is inevitable.
John F. Kennedy[1]

The last ten years of America's history have seen the development of a full-scale social movement for desegregation. Sporadic terrorism, rioting, and new federal laws occasionally give society some indication of the transformation under way in our polity. For the most part, the major portion of the population does not realize the significance of the change now taking place because their exposure to it has been indirect. Thus far our democratic institutions, although somewhat belatedly, have been able to accommodate desired change without chaos. Whether they will be able to do so in the years ahead depends upon what techniques civil rights organizations employ to realize future goals.

This chapter shows the ever changing nature of the civil rights movement. The sit-in movement of 1960 marked another turning point in the African American's fight for equality. It signified the initiation of a new wave of African American protest, the repercussions of which are still being felt. The political potential of the movement was dramatically registered for the first time when John F. Kennedy intervened on behalf of the Reverend Martin Luther King, Jr., who had been arrested for refusing to leave a table in a restaurant in Atlanta, Georgia.

---

1 Whitney M. Young, Jr., *To Be Equal* (New York: McGraw-Hill Good Company, 1964), p.241. Young quotes John F. Kennedy when speaking about the Alliance for Progress.

One cannot identify in the narrowness of American voting in 1960 any one particular episode or decision as being more important than any other in the final tallies; yet when one reflects that Illinois was carried by only 9,000 votes and that 250,000 Negroes are estimated to have voted for Kennedy; that Michigan was carried by 67,000 votes and that an estimated 250,000 Negroes voted for Kennedy; that South Carolina was carried by 10,000 votes and that an estimated 40,000 Negroes there voted for Kennedy, the candidate's instinctive decision must be ranked among the most crucial of the last few weeks.[2]

Initial campaigns for civil rights were directed primarily by members of the middle class and of the student population. In the course of integrating such middle class institutions as suburban housing and public swimming pools, additional people were needed to make the protests more effective. The expansion of membership brought more working class and unemployed people into the movement. This new composition in membership had three important results.

First, instead of the integration of country clubs, these people demanded things that would more readily improve their standard of living, such as jobs, housing, and schools.

Secondly, because the civil rights movement now concerns itself with issues that confront all Americans, it moves beyond the relationship between ethnic groups and deals instead with the relationship between the decision making processes of society and all men. African American political activity is becoming a very important factor in elections at all levels of government. A gradual evolution has occurred whereby the civil rights movement has changed from merely a vehicle of protest to a genuine social movement. Although it initially used such devices as sit-ins and freedom rides, it is now employing economic boycotts, rent strikes, community organization, and political action.

Lastly, an alteration in the membership of civil rights organizations has brought people into the movement who are more likely to employ violence as a tactic than are the middle class persons. Thirty-one year old Woodrow Coleman, an unemployed construction worker and member of the Nonviolent Action Committee, thinks that violence is inevitable:

---

2   Theodore H. White, *The Making of the President 1960* (New York: Pocket Books, Incorporated, 1962), p. 387.

"... We won't get a solution until we put (on) enough pressure, until the politicians realize that there's not going to be any peace until the Negroes get their freedom... The movement will probably come to bloodshed. We've tried enough non-violence and seen that it doesn't work."[3]

What has appeared in the last ten years, as far as the civil rights movement is concerned, is a shift in emphasis from the legalistic, courtroom approach made famous by the NAACP to the direct actionist, street approach employed by the SCLC, CORE, and SNCC. Today another shift is taking place, and the movement has reached a new and different phase. The actionist civil rights organizations are moving into the urban ghettos of the North and the rural hamlets of the South to develop community organizations that will employ political power to fulfill the people's needs and desires. At the same time the ballot finally is being recognized by most civil rights groups as the primary tool with which to produce change in a democratic society, some extreme civil rights organizations are advocating the use of violence if all else fails. These groups feel that the majority will only come to understand the plight of the minority through shocking and distasteful tactics.

Types of African American Protest Organizations

The current metamorphosis in the civil rights movement is actually just a mirror of the emergence, over a period of time, of five types of African American protest organizations: legal, educational, direct actionist, separatist, and extremist. Each group may be classified on the basis of the major strategy it employs to realize desired objectives:

1. Legal (NAACP)—"appeal to law through filing suits, court litigation, encouraging favorable legislation, and the like."[4]
2. Educational (Urban League)—"appeal to reason through researching, informing, consulting, persuading and negotiating with political and economic leaders." [5]
3. Direct Actionist (SCLC, CORE, and SNCC)—"appeal to morality through direct personal confrontation of the enforcers and tacit

---

3   Clay Carson, "Faces of Protest" Woody Coleman, *Los Angeles Sentinel*, June 18, 1965, p. 4.
4   James H. Laue, *The Changing Character of African American Protest*, *The Annals of the American Academy of Political and Social Science*, CCCLVII (January, 1965), 121.
5   Ibid., pp. 121-122.

bystanders of the segregated system, usually through non-violent direct action."[6]

4. Separatists (Black Muslims)—demand absolute separation of black and white races.

5. Extremists (Deacons for Defense and Justice)—a reliance on "defensive" violence as a retaliatory weapon against white terrorists and oppressors.

These organizations are not all-inclusive; rather, they overlap and continuously influence one another. The very proliferation of African American leadership groups indicates that, until recently, the African American revolution lacked a concrete direction. No one organization or leader speaks for all African Americans. With so many groups in the civil rights movement, it is only natural that there has been some competition among them for recognition, financial support, and how best to conduct the struggle in order to secure desired objectives. In a society as heterogeneous and diverse as America, it logically follows that there will be several personal approaches to a problem as complicated as civil rights. No one organization can fight discrimination and segregation alone because it cannot employ all the tactics necessary to overcome these social evils. A number of specialized groups, each focusing on specific aspects of the problems can meet with far more success.

The current civil rights movement is directed not only against that part of the white power structure that supports and maintains segregation, but also against the older, more conservative African American organizations and their leadership. Remembering this and keeping the aforementioned "multiple approach" to African American protest groups in mind, a frame of reference is now available which will allow analysis of the various civil rights organizations. They will be described by using a systematic framework that includes the following components: history, goals, organization, leadership and membership, and strategy and tactics.

Figure 7 indicates the approximate ideological position of each organization within the movement. Using the previously mentioned strategy classification of protest organizations, the gradual emergence of political power and "defensive violence" as the latest tools in the African American's fight for freedom become evident.

---

6   Ibid., p. 122.

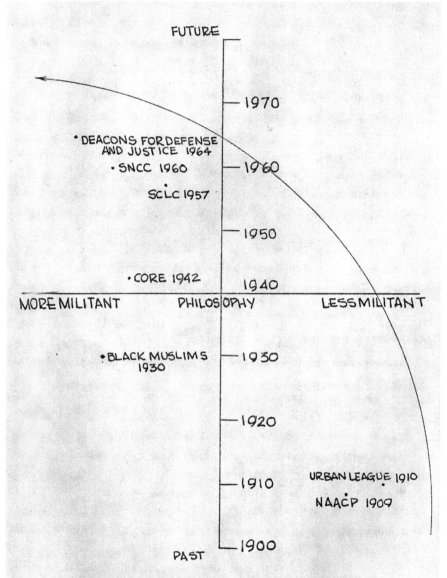

FUTURE

─ 1970

• DEACONS FOR DEFENSE
AND JUSTICE 1964
• SNCC 1960 ─ 1960
SCLC 1957

─ 1950

• CORE 1942 ─ 1940

MORE MILITANT   PHILOSOPHY   LESS MILITANT

• BLACK MUSLIMS ─ 1930
1930

─ 1920

─ 1910   URBAN LEAGUE 1910
•
NAACP 1909

─ 1900
PAST

FIGURE 7

ORGANIZATION-CHANGE MODEL

85

The Urban League

An interracial organization, the National Urban League developed out of a coalition of three social agencies in 1910 in New York City. The organization was comprised of philanthropists, professionals, and social workers who felt "that the Negro needed not alms but opportunity—opportunity to work at the job for which the Negro was best fitted, with equal pay for equal work, and opportunity for advancement."[7] While providing other services, the League's primary goal has been the securing of jobs for African Americans.

The league has branches in seventy cities, and five regional offices coordinate and supervise the programs of these local affiliates. Every local branch has a voluntary board of directors that is interracial. The League has a well-trained national staff and a cadre of full-time professional local directors. Six hundred paid staff members carry on day-to-day affairs, while more than 6,000 volunteers serve in the capacity of board and committee members.

The executive director of this body is Whitney M. Young, Jr., a forty-three year old African American who has given the League constructive and imaginative leadership since he took over on October 1, 1961. He received his Master's Degree from the University of Minnesota in social work in 1948. Before coming to the League he was Dean of the Atlanta University School of Social Work. Young has steered the organization toward a more militant course, participating in both the march on Washington and a voter registration drive.

The Urban League is the only civil rights group that has no serious financial problems. It planned to raise almost two million dollars in 1965, and its strong monetary position is due to the fact that much of the League's budget comes from United Funds and the Community Chest. In addition, it receives financial support from foundations, federal grants, wealthy black and white businessmen, labor unions, and corporations.

The Urban League employs a five-pronged attack to eliminate discrimination against the African American and to aid him in obtaining first class citizenship. First of all it defines the problem, and then it seeks to motivate youth. The third step takes the form of finding jobs and increasing employment. Next, it seeks to improve housing conditions, and lastly, attempts to see that African Americans are provided with adequate health and welfare services.

---

7   Arnold Rose, *The African American in America: The Condensed Version of Gunnar Myrdal's An American Dilemma* (New York: Harper and Row, 1964), p. 267.

The Urban League has lost a great deal of respect among African Americans over the years because it did not assault segregation in the visible fashion that other direct action groups did. However, it is unlikely that the goals it seeks to accomplish could be attained in any other fashion. Its programs and procedures may not be as colorful and spectacular as other civil rights groups; nevertheless, they are very important because they are assisting in the elimination of the very conditions that produce poverty and discontent among African Americans.

National Association for the Advancement of Colored People

The year 1905 saw the birth of the first aggressive African American action organization, the Niagara Movement, under the leadership of W.E.B. DuBois. Although this group met annually, its efforts yielded few results. Then, in 1908, a race riot occurred in Springfield, Illinois, in which many African Americans were killed, hurt, or driven permanently from their homes. The affair was given wide publicity and three people decided to do something about the poor plight of the African American. Mary White Ovington, William English Walling, and Dr. Henry Moskowitz met in New York in January 1909 and laid the plans for what was to become a new organization. In May 1910 white liberals in the abolitionist tradition and African American liberals in the Niagara Movement united and organized a permanent body known as the National Association for the Advancement of Colored People. The principal goal of this group is "to end racial segregation and all other forms of discrimination in all public aspects of American life."[8]

The NAACP actually is not one, but two organizations: the NAACP, led by executive secretary Roy Wilkins; and the NAACP Legal Defense and Educational Fund, directed by Jack Greenberg. The organization was separated in 1939 for tax purposes. The primary function of the Legal Defense and Educational Fund is to provide legal redress; consequently, contributions to it are tax deductible. On the other hand, the NAACP carries on political activity and maintains a lobby in Washington, and thus contributions to it are not tax deductible.

At the annual convention, attended by delegates from the various NAACP local units, policies that direct and guide the association are developed. The NAACP is governed by a Board of Directors, forty-two of

---

8   NAACP, *This Is the NAACP* (New York: NAACP, 1964), p.1.

whom are elected by local branches and the remaining eighteen by the Board itself. The Board convenes monthly. It has to review all resolutions passed by delegates and make a decision as to whether or not they will become a matter of organizational policy. A two-thirds vote against a resolution by the Board will kill it. However, a majority vote of the branches can override the Board's negative vote. The Board also appoints the executive secretary and confirms staff recommendations made by the executive secretary. The executive secretary and his staff are responsible for executing policies of the convention and of the Board. The NAACP program is carried out by volunteer personnel at the state and local levels.

The NAACP blankets the nation with between 1,500 and 1,700 chapters (exact figures vary). In addition to the national headquarters staff in New York, a Washington Bureau, two voter registration offices and sixteen field and regional offices exist to serve all local branches. Membership in 1964 stood at 462,000, which is 70,000 fewer members that in 1963. However, the organization explains that this decrease was due to the fact that it concentrated most of its energies on passage of the Civil Rights Act and on defeating Barry Goldwater for President. As a result, they say, it was inevitable that membership should suffer.

The organization operated on a budget of slightly over one million dollars in 1964. The NAACP relies heavily upon membership dues to fulfill its financial needs. Membership losses hurt the NAACP and it spent four hundred thousand dollars more in 1964 than it took in. Officials of the group say, however, that three hundred thousand dollars of this deficit is redeemable bail money.

The NAACP employs four major strategies to realize its objectives:

1. It uses the courts of the land, state and federal, to secure justice and level Jim Crow barriers.
2. It works for enactment of laws at national, state and local levels to protect civil rights and ban racial discrimination.
3. It carries on an educational program in efforts to create a climate of opinion in favor of equal rights and human brotherhood.
4. It also engages in selective buying campaigns, picketing and direct action programs.[9]

It is no accident that legal activities are listed as the NAACP's first tool in reaching its goals, nor direct action as the last weapon it employs. The

---

9   Ibid., p. 2.

NAACP frequently has been called "the world's biggest law firm." For many years of its history it literally represented all the African Americans in the United States. In the early years of the civil rights struggle the legal process was the primary tool for social change. In 1915 the NAACP participated in its first Supreme Court case. It won a decision that outlawed the "grandfather clause" in the Constitution of the state of Oklahoma.[10] More recently the NAACP won what is considered its most outstanding legal victory when the Supreme Court ruled that the doctrine of "separate but equal" had no place in public education in 1954.[11] Such legal successes have facilitated the African American's progress in America and have given the organization much stature and support.

When, in the mid 1950's and very early 1960's, the civil rights revolution began to grow more militant, the NAACP and its legalistic approach began to fade.

> The NAACP's troubling is born of the fact that the events of the past three years have shaken our faith in legalism as a tool for deliverance; we now want our major civil rights organizations to look beyond the courts to the people themselves as the final and quick arbiters of public policy.[12]

As custodian of the civil rights movement, the NAACP leadership has been rather slow in supporting direct action tactics. The executive director of the NAACP, Roy Wilkins, has said:

> "(They) furnish the noise" in the racial protests while the NAACP "pays the bills," Wilkins said of CORE, SNCC, and SCLC, "here today and gone tomorrow. There is only one organization that can handle a long, sustained fight—the NAACP."[13]

When the NAACP held its fifty-sixth Annual Convention in Denver, Colorado this year, internal dissension within the ranks of the organization was exposed when a group of "young Turks" stated that the attempt to switch the 1966 convention site from Los Angeles to Birmingham was just

---

10 Guinn v. United States, 238 U.S. 347; 35 S. Ct. 926; 59 L.Ed. 1340 (1915).

11 Brown v. Board of Education of Topeka, 347 U.S. 483; 74 S. Ct. 686; 98 L.Ed. 873 (1954).

12 Louis E. Lomax, *The African American Revolt* (New York: The New American Library of World Literature, Incorporated, 1963), p. 132.

13 William Brink and Louis Harris, *The African American Revolution in America* (New York: Simon and Schuster, 1964), p.43.

a power play by conservatives who control the civil rights group. According to them:

> ...the change was suggested to ease criticism by many Negroes who claim the NAACP has become overly concerned with the accomplishments of the past and has failed to provide any dynamic leadership in the civil rights struggle.[14]

Many in the NAACP want to cooperate more with other civil rights groups. In addition, these same people want to take a more militant stand so as to keep pace in the direct action field. One of the "young Turks," Jack Tanner, had this to say about the future of the NAACP: "Unless the leadership of the NAACP recognizes that a more forceful approach must be used in the civil rights battle, the organization will wither away and lose all influence within the Negro population."[15]

At the present time it appears that the leadership of the NAACP, while recognizing that the demonstration still has a limited function, will rely on the ballot to carry the African American's cause forward. Emphasis will be placed on using the political process to implement existing legislation and to become part of the decision making power structure. According to Edward A. Hailes, Executive Director of the Washington, D.C. branch of the NAACP, "you're going to see a lot of activity in the political arena by Negroes, not only in voter registration but in teaching Negroes the value of the ballot."[16]

The Southern Christian Leadership Conference

From its very inception, and until very recently, the NAACP has placed primary emphasis on legal redress activities. Consequently, when the African American lost faith in the white power structure and its institutions, he lost faith in the groups that used conventional means to fight segregation and discrimination. As a result, some organization(s) had to emerge to fill the leadership vacuum and take the African American masses beyond legalism to action. Three comparatively new organizations took over the leadership

---

14   Paul Beck, "Attempt to Move 1966 Convention from L.A. Discloses NAACP Rift," *The Los Angeles Times*, July 1, 1965, p.1.

15   Ibid., p.16.

16   Paul Beck, "NAACP Leaders Report African American Big City Gains," *The Los Angeles Times*, July 5, 1965, p. 2.

mantle and stepped to the forefront of the African American revolt: SCLC, CORE, [17] and SNCC.

The Southern Christian Leadership Conference grew out of the Montgomery Improvement Association, which was formed to carry on a boycott against segregated local bus lines in Montgomery, Alabama. After the boycott was terminated successfully, many wondered if this type of activity could be carried on throughout the entire South. A meeting took place on January 10-11, 1957 in Atlanta, and the SCLC was born. A functional structure was developed and the Reverend Dr. Martin Luther King, Jr., who was to become the acknowledged leader and most respected spokesman of the African American revolution, was elected president.

The aims and purpose of the SCLC are:

1. To achieve full citizenship rights, and total integration of the African American in American life.
2. To stimulate nonviolent direct mass action to remove the barriers of segregation and discrimination.
3. To disseminate the creative philosophy and techniques of non-violence through local and area workshops.
4. To secure the right and unhampered use of the ballot for every citizen.
5. To reduce the cultural lag through the Citizenship Training Program.[18]

An Executive Board meets twice a year to set policy, and a convention convenes annually for legislative and inspirational purposes. The Reverend Wyatt T. Walker, SCLC's executive director, is responsible for day-to-day decision making. Under his direction the staff has increased from six to sixty-one. Moreover, the SCLC has a complete cadre of field secretaries, regional directors, secretaries, and clerks.

The SCLC is an affiliate rather than a membership organization. It is composed of approximately 100 church, civic, and related groups in thirty states that engage in fund raising, for the most part. The theory behind this affiliate type of organization is that, with the guidance and influence of Martin Luther King and the SCLC, clerics in the South will be able to assume the responsibility for civil rights leadership in their cities and carry any protest to a successful conclusion. The SCLC has met with some success in this area,

---

17 See Chapter III for discussion of CORE and its effect on the civil rights movement.
18 Ed Clayton (editor), *The SCLC Story* (Atlanta: SCLC, 1964), p.14.

although it has neither established a complete grass roots organization in the South nor has it eliminated discrimination entirely.

The story of the SCLC is really the story of Martin Luther King. Created by the African American revolution, the thirty-seven year old Baptist minister is now the titular head of the current civil rights movement and the most famous African American leader in America. His home has been bombed three times, he has been stabbed in the chest, and he has been jailed on fourteen occasions.[19] In addition to being the author of a number of best selling books on civil rights and the recipient of a Nobel Prize, he travels 325,000 miles a year to make speeches on behalf of the African American's cause and to raise money for SCLC (he often collects as much as ten thousand dollars for a single appearance). Besides being the initial disciple of the nonviolent approach to civil rights in America, Martin Luther King's greatest contribution has been that of raising hope for the millions of oppressed Southern African Americans. During the Selma to Montgomery march Frank Haralson, a sixty-two year old African American resident, was asked when he first heard of Martin Luther King.

> "In 'fifty-five, when he started the bus boycott, I workin' there in Montgomery in a chair factory at the time. I had transportation, and I picket up many people on the streets. The people practical give up, but they hold out."[20]

During the same march Mrs. Mary Jane Jackson, seventy-three years of age and an African American, said the first time she heard of Martin Luther King,

> "...was when they bomb his house. Then I always love to hear his name called and look at his picture, because I hear nice things about him. I believe God like him, too."[21]

Segregation is on its death bed, and Martin Luther King and his efforts have assisted greatly in putting it there.

---

19   "Playboy Interview: Martin Luther King, a Candid Conversation with the Nobel Prize-Winning Leader of the Civil Rights Movement,," *Playboy*, XII (January, 1965), 65.

20   W. C. Heinz and Bard Lindeman, "The Meaning of the Selma March: Great Day at Trickem Fork," *Post*, May 22, 1965, p. 92.

21   Ibid., p.90.

The SCLC relies heavily on nonviolent direct action to accomplish its goals. Operating throughout the South, SCLC does not move into a problem area until a request for its services is received from one of its affiliate organizations. In the early 1960's it began to supplement its direct action tactics with voter registration campaigns that covered the area from Virginia to Texas. In addition, it has developed citizenship education and voter registration schools. Operating in six Southern states, SCOPE (Southern Community Organization and Political Education), SCLC's summer voting program, was "designed to liberalize the political philosophy of at least 12 congressional districts and to assume the election of African Americans or right thinking whites to more than 72 state representative and senatorial positions in the six states."[22] Although initial success was not as great as expected, such political activity is bound to break the white man's hold on politics in the South in the near future.

Student Nonviolent Coordination Committee

No organization demonstrates the changing nature of the civil rights movement more than does *Snick*. Snick was born out of the student sit-ins that began in 1960 in Greensboro, North Carolina. A temporary committee to promote communication and coordination of activities among the various protest groups was established and an office was opened in Atlanta, after a meeting of all sit-in leaders was held in Raleigh, North Carolina. In October 1960 another conference was held, and SNCC was established formally. Realizing the plight of the rural, Southern African American, Snick made an important change in their direct action strategy and decided to carry the civil rights movement to the South's Black Belt via voter education and voter registration in 1961.

Snick's goals reflect the integrated approach to the African American's fight for civil rights. Employing both direct action and political activity, they want to continue:

1. introducing educated and determined young workers into hard core areas.
2. maintaining a college contact that leads to militant action in cities and provides new recruits for full time work.

---

22   Jack Nelson, "Dixie Political Revolt Begins," *The Los Angeles Times*, August 8, 1965, p.2.

3. expanding our pilot voter registration projects in cities to provide workers in surrounding counties.
4. finding more funds to support students willing to work at subsistence wages and share the life of the Southern rural African American while trying to convince him of his rights.
5. providing more and better workshops and conferences on the meaning and techniques of nonviolent community action and political involvement.[23]

Like the SCLC, Snick is not a membership organization. It is an association that endeavors to encourage and spread the growth of local protest movements. A coordinating Committee, composed of members of various protest groups, meets on a regular basis to develop strategy. "The committee elects an executive committee, which is responsible for employing staff and overseeing the general programs."[24]

Snick's staff has doubled in the past year and it now totals 220 people. Of these, 140 are African American. The average staff worker's age is twenty-two. Snick personnel receive a basic wage of only twenty dollars a week. In addition to the staff, Snick has about 300 volunteers in the field this summer who received no pay. The majority of Snick's one million dollar budget comes from the Friends of SNCC, a group of 150 chapters located on college campuses and in cities in the North.

Although an anti-leader organization, Snick has two men who hold this rather amorphous body together. The first one is James Forman, Snick's executive secretary. At thirty-six, he brings a great deal of experience and maturity to the movement, and is partially responsible for Snick's activity to redistribute political power in the South. Snick's chairman is John Lewis. At twenty-five, he is one of the youngest higher echelon officials in the civil rights movement. Beaten twelve times and arrested on thirty-eight occasions, he personifies the personal sacrifices necessary to obtain full equality for the African American. In the North he is much in demand on the fund raising circuits.

Snick wants to restructure America along lines that are more egalitarian and proletarian. To accomplish this end they are employing a grass roots strategy that is designed to build indigenous, trained leadership that will help the African American to help himself and give him a voice in his own

---

23 SNCC, *SNCC* (Atlanta, SNCC, 1963), p. 4.
24 Ibid., p.5.

destiny. This strategy currently is being implemented by persuading every African American in the South to vote through such devices as the Mississippi Summer Project and the Mississippi Freedom Democratic party.

Snick is concentrating its efforts in Mississippi, where it hopes to see a political realignment take place. It has organized a political party (FDP) that has a state committee, county chairmen, and precinct leaders. "With the coming of real voting rights, F.D.P. will change from a training school to the most powerful African American organization in Mississipi."[25] The FDP, unlike the regular Democratic Party of Mississippi, supported the national Democratic ticket in the 1964 Presidential election, challenged the loyalty and credentials of the official delegates to the Democratic National Convention, and requested that they be seated instead. They attempted to unseat Mississippi's five congressmen, contending that they were elected illegally because African Americans were denied the right to vote. If past activity is any indication of FDP's future, as soon as increased African American registration takes effect many local, state, and federal political offices are bound to pass into hands that are more friendly to African Americans.

Black Muslims

Some civil rights organizations are not content to reach their goals within the framework of American society. Instead of working toward an integrated society, they would rather sever all ties with white America and establish their own state. Such a separatist organization is the Black Muslims.

The Black Muslims were founded by a mysterious peddler named W.D. Fard in Detroit in 1930. Preaching about the deceptive nature of the white man and about the glorious history of Black Afro-Asia, Fard established an effective organization in three years. In 1934 Fard disappeared and Elijah Muhammad took over as the Prophet and Messenger of Allah. Under Muhammad the Muslims have prospered. His leadership has seen the development of a number of temples and schools, and the acquisition of a variety of apartment houses, farms, grocery stores, and restaurants. Even more significant, however, is the fact that "he has given them a new sense of dignity, a conviction that they are more than the equal of the white man and are destined to rule the earth."[26]

---

25   Richard Armstrong, "Will Snick Overcome?" *Post*, August 28, 1965, p. 82.
26   C. Eric Lincoln, *The Black Muslims in America* (Boston: Beacon Press, 1963), pp. 16-17.

The Black Muslims have three basic objectives: (1) a united front of black men, (2) racial separation, and (3) economic separation. They feel that the white man's greatest fear is black unity. Hence the reason for goal number one. The Muslims want complete separation between the black and white ethnic groups because they feel that there is no reason to integrate with a dying world:

> ...Today's world is floating in corruption; its complete disintegration is both imminent and inescapable. Any man who integrates with the world must share in its disintegration and destruction. If the Black Man would but listen he need not be a part of this certain doom.[27]

Economically, the Muslims also want total separation from the white man because they feel that his economic dominance gives him the power to control the lives of the African Americans. How fast the economic withdrawal can be accomplished depends upon how fast black businesses and industries can be established.

The Muslims, a nationwide organization, claim 100,000 militant "Black Men." (*Time* magazine feels that approximately 10,700 would be a closer estimate of their actual strength.) [28] As of December 1960 the organization had sixty-nine temples in twenty-seven states. The Muslims are ruled by an authoritarian leader and have no rigidly structured chain of command. Before his assassination, Malcolm X was Muhammad's side. However, Malcolm gained such popularity that he actually became a threat to Elijah Muhammad's leadership and was expelled from the organization. Raymond Sharrieff, Muhammad's son-in-law and chief aide, manages the Muslim's commercial enterprises and directs the Fruit of Islam (FOI), the Muslim security corps and enforcement elite. Others near the center of power are Ministers Louis X of Boston, Lucius X of Washington, D.C., Isaiah Karriem of Baltimore, and Wilfred X of Detroit. Lottie X, the movement's most important woman, heads the Muslim Girls Training Class (MGT), the counterpart of the FOI.

The Muslim rank and file is made up predominately of young African American males who belong to the lower classes and who are now ex-Christians. The organization is financed by the membership. Each adherent pays slightly over eight dollars per week in dues and is required to sell or pay for as many as 200 copies of the Muslim newspaper, *Mr. Muhammad Speaks,*

---

27   Ibid., p. 89.
28   "Races, Death and Transfiguration,," *Time*, LXXXV (March 5, 1965), 23-25.

every two weeks. In addition, on February 26, Savior's Day, every member has to pay an assessment of one hundred twenty-five dollars.

The Black Muslims engage in neither direct action activity nor voter education and registration drives. To achieve their ultimate goal of a separate state for all African Americans, they emphasize economic independence. Muslims are encouraged to "buy black." The organization itself owns and operates small businesses; and an intensive recruitment drive is conducted, often among the less desirable elements of society, so that more adherents will join the movement and aid the sect's desire for black supremacy.

The Black Muslims believe in an "eye for an eye and a tooth for a tooth." Followers of Muhammad are instructed that they are not to initiate violence, but they are to strike back if they are attacked. The nonviolent philosophy of Martin Luther King has no place in this organization. In fact:

> ...the Movement is temperamentally extremist. It is balanced precariously at the very edge of the spectrum, at the farthest extreme from the serene near docility of the Negro Church. If the movement becomes significantly more extreme—and this is a possibility that must be reckoned with—it will no longer be expressing simple protest. It will have crossed the line to open and violent rebellion.[29]

The Deacons for Defense and Justice

James Forman once said that "you don't get change without some breakage."[30] A number of African Americans now feel that nonviolence, as a strategy in the civil rights movement, has failed to alleviate the African American's inferior position in society. One such group, advocating arming for "defensive purposes," is the Deacons for Defense and Justice. They feel weapons are necessary because Southern law enforcement and justice for the African American are nonexistent. Apparently Martin Luther King was right when he stated that "violence grows to the degree that injustice prevails; the more injustice in a given community, the more violence, or potential violence, smolders in that community."[31]

The Deacons represent a new element in the civil rights struggle. The original chapter was founded in Jonesboro, Louisiana, in the fall of 1964. Since then the Deacons have grown to fifty-five chapters, with between 5,000

---

29   Lincoln, op. cit., p. 248.
30   Armstrong, loc. cit., p.80.
31   "Playboy Interview...," loc.cit., p.73.

and 15,000 members in Louisiana, Mississippi, and Alabama. Fund raising units are in the process of being established in New York, San Francisco, and other large cities. A ladies auxiliary, the Deaconesses, has also been formed, and they participate in activities like target practice alongside the men.

Feeling that it takes violence to counteract violence, the Deacons explain that their sole goal is to protect African Americans and civil rights workers from attacks by the armed racists. The Deacons have a parent organization that receives one hundred dollars from each local chapter and 10 percent of the chapter's dues. The parent group assists in equipping local chapters with two-way radio equipment. Chapter initiation fees are ten dollars and dues are two dollars per month. Intercity radio communications allow chapters to call each other for reinforcements in case of an emergency. Weekly meetings are held to exchange data on any harassment by whites or law enforcement offices of African Americans or civil rights workers.

The strategy of the Deacons is essentially counter intimidation. It appears to have met with some success, as the Deacons already have been involved in two shooting incidents with raiding white racists. Ernest Thomas, one of the organizers of the order, feels that the Deacons actually have assisted in keeping down racial violence.

The chapter that has implemented this philosophy of *defensive violence* most aggressively is the one located in Bogalusa, Louisiana. It is headed by forty-one-year-old Charles Sims. Containing between 175 and 200 men, many of them former armed services veterans, the chapter is fully equipped with radios, walkie talkies, grenades, gas bombs, and M-1 rifles. The Deacons have set up a patrol system in the African American community to protect the residents of the area from any possible white hostility.

The growth of this African American vigilante group has brought mixed reactions from other civil rights leaders. Martin Luther Kind is strongly opposed to the use of violence in any form because he feels that the aim of the civil rights movement should be to convert, not annihilate, the opponents of equality for all. Bayard Rustin, executive director of the A. Philip Randolph Institute, has stated that he is:

> ...against armed defense on either side. An organized army brings in an element which is basically disorderly. If any groups require protection, it

is a police problem and if southern police are not prepared to deal with it, we should ask for federal police intervention.[32]

On the other hand, James Farmer, national director of CORE, has defended the Deacons. In fact, his organization helped formulate the Bogalusa chapter and now works openly with them. The turn toward violence and the birth of a group like the Deacons probably was best summed up by John Lewis of SNCC when he said: "Resistance on the part of certain Southern cities and outright violence by groups like the Ku Klux Klan will determine the degree that we will have groups like the Deacons."[33]

32 Jack Nelson, "Arming of Negroes in Rights Fight Assailed," *The Los Angeles Times*, June 15, 1965, p.5.
33 "Civil Rights: The Deacons," *Newsweek*, LXVI (August 2, 1965), 29.

Reformation: from Protest to Persuasive Politics and Violence

One of the most unique characteristics of the present civil rights revolution is the speed with which the center of the movement is becoming alienated from traditional American middle class values of respectability. The NAACP and Roy Wilkins have yielded the stage to the SCLC and Martin Luther King, who was considered by most whites to be a radical extremist as little as five years ago. Dr. King, in turn, has yielded the center to James Farmer of CORE and James Foreman of SNCC, who both use a very aggressive form of nonviolence. From here there are two remaining positions, both of them currently emerging and tenable, for the civil rights movement to take.

The first is violence, whether of the *defensive* kind employed by Deacons in Louisiana or the *destructive* type used by the African Americans rioting in the Los Angeles ghetto area of Watts. African American violence can stem from a spontaneous eruption of emotion or from lower class members of the group who do not have a vested interest in the status quo and who feel alienated from society. No matter what the source the final result can be only be repression, even though there may now be a greater awareness on the part of society as to the African American's plight, because the state is the only institution that has a monopoly on the legitimate use of force and it will not hesitate to use it if it feels that society is threatened. "You do not solve social problems with violence—you only vent anger."[34]

Another alternative toward which the civil rights movement can advance is increased peaceful political activity. All signs to date seem to indicate that the movement is converging on the ballot.[35] In fact, "the single greatest challenge to Negro leadership is to realize the political potential of the Negro at the polls."[36] As yet, African Americans have failed to get out of the political process what other minorities have managed to obtain because many whites have successfully discouraged the majority of African Americans from participating in politics. Nevertheless, a turn toward political action is

---

34   "Wilkins Sees Good, Bad in Wake of L.A. Rioting," *The Los Angeles Times*, October 27, 1965, p.3.

35   Bayard Rustin, *From Protest to Politics: The Future of the Civil Rights Movement*, *Commentary*, XXXIX (February, 1965), 25-31.

36   Brink and Harris, op. cit., p.82.

definitely under way, and what started as a protest movement is gradually transforming itself into a political movement.

Many leaders feel that they can best employ the African American's potential political power by forming an African American-labor-liberal axis that would work as a coalition toward desired goals. Others feel that African Americans should work solely within the framework of the Democratic Party because this is the only political organization that has been at all responsive to the African American's cause in recent years. Finally, there are those who insist that the African American community should not be in the "hip pocket" of any political party. These people agree with James Farmer, who has called for the organization of a African American party that would function apart from the Republican or Democratic Parties. Farmer feels that African Americans need independent political voices that can be heard in the North as well as in the South. He wants CORE to take the lead in establishing political movements in the ghetto communities that will enable African Americans to better their position in society. In Farmer's opinion, CORE is the only organization that can organize the African Americans adequately because it has a nationwide network of militant chapters, and it alone has the flexibility needed for this phase of the civil rights movement.

Regardless of the vehicle chosen, it is readily apparent that the use of political power by African Americans is going to make big differences in the North and in the South. American politics are bound to undergo some fundamental changes as more and more African Americans register and become politically mature. In fact:

> The future of the Negro revolution depends in large part on how many Negroes will fight through the impediments to registration and how many will come to cast their ballots in every election from now on. Success in these two areas will determine whether or not the Negro's potential power...is realized.[37]

---

37   <u>Ibid</u>., p.95.

CHAPTER V
Concluding Generalizations

Among the great movements of the twentieth century, the one likely to have the most significant impact on American society is the civil rights movement. Beginning with the Montgomery bus boycott in 1955, the country has passed through domestic revolution of violence and hostility the likes which have not been known since the Civil War. Very few social problems in the nation's history have given the country the challenge and the opportunity that the civil rights struggle now presents. As far as the African American is concerned, "America is free to choose whether the Negro shall remain her liability or become her opportunity."[1]

The concluding statements to be presented here are merely generalizations. In a movement that is constantly altering, factual statements are often difficult to make because of the very uncertain nature of this dynamic force as it relates to a changing society.

The Civil Rights Movement

1. The Civil rights movement is essentially revolutionary in that it demands drastic changes in the present patterns of American life.
   A. It emphasizes that the changes it wants are drastic in nature.
   B. It believes the changes it desires, although revolutionary, are in accord with the democratic creed of freedom, equality, and justice for all.

---

1   "New Crisis: The African American Family," *Newsweek*, LXVI (August 9, 1965), 35.

2. The failure of the legal process in many of the Southern states has led to the development and growth of the civil rights movement and to continuously changing forms of direct action protest.

   A. The refusal of many young African Americans to accept the indignities that their parents suffered at the hands of whites has been a contributory condition to the rise of African American protest.

3. The civil rights movement has become the vehicle by which the despair of many African Americans has been channelized into purposeful action.

   A. The motivating agent in this social movement is shared anger.

   B. The weapons of this movement are sit-ins, boycotts, demonstrations, picket lines, and the ballot.

   C. This social movement has enabled many African Americans to achieve an identity, to feel a sense of "somebodiness."

4. The civil rights movement has been constructed around just one issue: equality for the African American.

   A. The vast majority of its supporters are people concerned solely with civil rights.

   B. This has become the movement's primary liability because it has not built an organization that is stable and disciplined and that has a broad basis of support among the masses.

   C. Its successes were achieved because of inept Southern officials and because of the supporting climate of an aroused public opinion, not because of a mass-based organization.

5. The civil rights movement failed to reach the uneducated masses in society until recent years.

   A. The focal points of action are fast becoming the local community in the Northern ghetto and the rural Southern town, where political action programs and remedial education campaigns are now being conducted.

6. The nearer a disadvantaged group gets to its goals, the more difficult it becomes to understand or explain the discrepancies that still remain.

   A. The closer the civil rights movement comes to obtaining its objective of full equality for all African Americans, the faster its impatience and bitterness increase.

7. The great allies of the civil rights movement have been those people who wish to maintain the status quo and who have resisted every attempt to improve the African American's status in America.
   A. The movement would never have been started if individuals like Sheriff Jim Clark of Selma, Alabama, had not removed or harassed civil rights leaders and organizers.
8. The civil rights movement has passed through the stages of social unrest and popular excitement. It is now approaching some degree of formalization.
   A. It has created and encouraged unity and pride in the race.
   B. It has mobilized public opinion, particularly in the North, to view the majority of its activities favorably.
   C. Its nonviolent direct action tactics have resulted in the passage of much favorable legislation.

The Los Angeles Chapter of the Congress of Racial Equality: A Case Study

Goals
1. "… The elimination of discrimination based on religion, race, skin color, or national origin in all phases at all levels of American life."[2]

Government and Organization
2. Essentially a "membership" rather than a leadership organization, operating somewhat like a committee of the whole.

Membership
3. Membership characteristics can be identified as follows:
   a. Composition is interracial.
   b. The vast majority of members are from the lower socio-economic level in our society.
   c. A low level of educational attainment is present among most members.
   d. Without exception, CORE members are affiliated with the Democratic Party.
   e. The membership as a whole is on the young side.

---

2   CORE, *Constitution of the Los Angeles Congress of Racial Equality*, (Los Angeles: CORE, 1963), Article II, p. 1. (Mimeographed)

4. At the present time there is a lack of a "sense of involvement" on the part of most members.

Finance

5. CORE suffers from a lack of funds with which to operate. Moreover, poor internal cost control procedures and poor fund raising activities make its financial position extremely weak.

Physical Plant

6. CORE's office, while functional, is inadequately maintained and is in a continuous state of disorder

Symbolism

7. Buttons and stickers provide distinctive symbols that identify the individual as a member of the group

Publications

8. The primary function of CORE publications is to keep the membership fully informed on all chapter activities. These publications fall into three categories:
    a. The monthly calendar
    b. Bulletins containing special announcements
    c. Political information sheets

Tactics

9. CORE uses the technique of nonviolent direct action as a primary weapon in the fight to overcome racial injustice

Conflict

10. If internal dissension and dissatisfaction ever hold away in a social movement, it is headed for obscurity
    a. "Cleavages" have and can split the chapter because there is an ever present dichotomy between the "more" militant faction and the "less" militant faction
    b. Inability to reach a consensus has seriously impaired CORE's effectiveness

Future

11. CORE is confronted with a number of problems, all of which have to be solved if it is to be a strong organization in the years ahead.

   a. Its future lies in the minority community, where it should make every effort to create programs, activities, and services of a self-help nature that will meet the interests and needs of the people living there.

   b. It should also devote time and energy to political education and voter registration in order to take greater advantage of the African American's potential political power in Los Angeles.

The Changing Nature of the Civil Rights Movement

Goal

1. The goal of the civil rights movement remains that of nothing less than total equality for the African American in every phase of American life

Multiple Approach

2. In a society as heterogeneous and diverse as America, it is only natural to expect that there will be several organizations working in the field of civil rights because the problem is so complicated.

Organizations

3. Civil rights organizations actually are small in size and power.

Leadership

4. No one single person acts as a leader of the civil rights movement; instead, there are several African Americans who occupy positions of power as leaders.

   a. Both legalistic and charismatic leaders are present, though the latter are most prevalent.

Membership

5. All social classes furnish members for the various protest organizations.

   a. The lower class African American, who is usually much more anti-white than the middle and upper class African Americans, has only recently begun to participate in civil rights organizations in an important way. His membership potential is high.

b. The economic gap between the lower and middle class African Americans is significant; consequently there is a grave danger that the middle class African American will not identify with or help the lower class African American. Instead, he will focus his attention, for the most part, on his own privileged class.

Finance

6. Every civil rights organization has a problem in securing adequate financial resources.

a. Fund raising will continue to be a problem as long as African Americans and white liberals fail to equalize their convictions with their financial contributions.

Politics

7. The civil rights movement is now turning to an essentially political phase.

a. Realizing that the morality of whites was not a sufficient condition with which to bring about a basic alteration in African American status, the movement went beyond love and began to seek political power.

b. As African Americans began to realize the uses that could be made of the political process, the more they began to desire political power.

c. Being a minority, the African Americans need allies in their struggle to win political power. The future should see some type of African American-labor-liberal axis developed for political purposes.

d. Possession of voting rights by the African American is a necessary condition for his acceptance as an equal citizen in American society.

e. Strength, not weakness, is a necessary condition for the achievement of full equality for the African American.

f. There will be a corresponding increase in the strength of the urban African American vote as more and more African Americans move into the metropolitan areas of the nation in the years ahead.

Violence

8. The civil rights movement is now characterized by a growing militancy on the part of many African Americans and whites currently associated with it.

    a. Disillusionment, due to inequities in the political process, is a contributory condition to the possibility of civil disorder within the society.

    b. Every significant social change is accompanied at some point by some degree of violence.

    c. A revolution cannot take place without conflict because a consensus cannot be reached before conflict takes place.

    d. If he were really a violent person, the African American would have been violent long ago.

The Normative Theory of Democracy and the African American

1. The existence of the normative theory of democracy is a necessary condition for African Americans to obtain power.

2. Peaceful, nonviolent direct action demonstrations indicate that most African Americans believe and trust in the democratic process.

3. Involuntary segregation is a sufficient condition to cause deprivation among a section of the population.

4. Favorable economic forces, such as high employment rates, an expanding economy, and increasing disposable income, are necessary conditions that should be present if the objectives of the civil rights movement are to be realized.

5. Favorable attitudes on the part of local and state officials are a necessary condition for the prevention of community upheaval when desegregation comes.

6. The purported existence of the normative theory of democracy is a sufficient condition to cause the majority of Americans to believe in the myth that the United States is the land of opportunity, generosity, and sympathy for all its citizens.

    a. Failure to adhere to democratic ideals in the North and the controlling by whites of economic and political power in the South has resulted in the failure of the realization of democratic ideals by all African Americans.

7. The attainment of educational opportunities is a necessary condition for the securing of economic, political, and social equality by African Americans.

From the above generalizations we can come to three broad conclusions suggested by the foregoing research:

1. The despair and frustrations which are behind any social movement have caused the African American to channel his protests into a civil rights movement.
2. After its start as a relatively moderate form of social protest, the civil rights movement has shifted toward increased political activity and even violence.
3. The divergence between the ideals of democracy and the realities of the African American's situation is diminishing in magnitude.

Suggestions for Further Study

The information presented in this study might be utilized as data for a longitudinal survey of the civil rights movement in 1970. A number of areas might be investigated as possible focal points for fruitful analysis:

1. Has the civil rights movement become completely formalized or institutionalized?
2. If so, what impact has this had on its leaders, followers, goals, strategy, and tactics?
3. What is the condition of the Los Angeles chapter of CORE with respect to the areas investigated in this study?
4. Has the civil rights movement been effective in the political arena?
5. Has violence on the part of African Americans completely disappeared or is it more in vogue than ever before?
6. Have segregation and discrimination been eliminated?
7. If so, how long did it take and what were the means by which this was finally accomplished?
8. Has the African American situation ceased to be a problem area in American Society and has it taken its place in history alongside such movements as the Populists and the Progressives, or is it still disrupting the national life?

BIBLIOGRAPHY

Books

Allport, Gordon W. *ABC's of Scapegoating.* New York: Anti-Defamation League of B'nai B'rith, 1948.

_____. *Prejudice in Modern Perspective.* Johannesburg: The South African Institute for Race Relations, 1956.

Baldwin, James. *Go Tell It on the Mountain.* New York: The New American Library of World Literature, Incorporated, 1963.

_____. *Nobody Knows My Name: More Notes of a Native Son.* New York: Dell Publishing Company, Incorporated, 1964.

_____. *The Fire Next Time.* New York: Dell Publishing Company, Incorporated, 1964.

Bardolph, Richard. *The Negro Vanguard.* New York: Alfred A. Knopf, Incorporated and Random House, Incorporated, a Vintage Book, 1961.

Barnett, H. G. *Innovation: The Basis of Cultural Change.* New York: McGraw-Hill Book Company, Incorporated, 1953.

Berry, Brewton. *Race and Ethnic Relations.* Boston: Houghton Mifflin Company, 1958.

Blumer, Herbert. *Collective Behavior,* in *New Outline of the Principles of Sociology.* Edited by Alfred McClung Lee. New York: Barnes and Noble, 1951.

Brink, William, and Louis Harris. *The Negro Revolution in America.* New York: Simon and Schuster, 1964.

Buckley, William F., Jr. *Civil Rights Must Not Destroy Liberty,* in *American*

Government: The Clash of Issues. Edited by J.A. Burhart, H.C. Bush, S. Krislov, and R.L. Lee. Englewood Cliffs, New Jersey: Prentice-Hall, Incorporated, 1964.

Cable, George W. *The Negro Question.* Edited by Arlin Turner, Garden City, New York: Doubleday and Company, Incorporated, 1958.

Canby, Henry Seidel. *Thoreau.* Boston: Houghton Mifflin Company, 1939.

Cantril, Hadley. *The Psychology of Social Movements.* New York: John Wiley and Son, Incorporated, 1941.

Chapman, John Jay. *Coatesville Address*, in *American Issues: A Sourcebook for Speech Topics.* Edited by Edwin Black and Harry P. Kerr. New York: Harcourt, Brace and World, Incorporated, 1961.

Clayton, Ed (editor). *THE SCLC Story.* Atlanta: SCLC, 1964.

Dawson, Carl A., and Warner E. Gettys. *An Introduction to Sociology.* New York: The Ronald Press Company, 1929.

Dawson, William L. *Segregation in the Armed Forces*, in *American Issues: A Sourcebook for Speech Topics.* Edited by Edwin Black and Harry P. Kerr. New York: Harcourt, Brace and World, Incorporated, 1961.

Drake, St. Clair, and Horace R. Cayton. *Black Metropolis: A Study of Negro Life in a Northern City.* Volumes I and II. New York: Harper Torchbook Edition, 1962.

Gandhi, M. K. *Non-Violence in Peace and War. Volume II.* Ahmedabad: Navajivan Publishing House, 1949.

Green, Arnold W. *Sociology, An Analysis of Life in Modern Society.* New York: McGraw Hill Book Company, Incorporated, 1960.

Greenberg, Jack. *Race Relations and American Law.* New York: Columbia University Press, 1959.

Griffin, John Howard. *Black Like Me.* New York: The New American Library of World Literature, Incorporated, 1964.

Harrington, Michael. *The Other America: Poverty in the United States.* Baltimore: Penguin Books, Incorporated, 1964.

Heberle, Rudolf. *Social Movements.* New York: Appleton-Century-Crofts, Incorporated, 1951.

Hentoff, Nat. *The New Equality.* New York The Viking Press, 1964.

Herskovits, Melville J. *Man and His Works.* New York: Alfred A. Knopf, 1949.

Hoffer, Eric. *The True Believer.* New York: The New American Library of World Literature, Incorporated, 1963.

Hofstadter, Richard. *The Age of Reform: From Bryan to F.D.R.* New York: Alfred A. Knopf, Incorporated and Random House, Incorporated, a Vintage Book, 1955.

Hughes, Langston. *Fight for Freedom.* New York: Berkley Publishing Corporation, 1962.

Hunter, Floyd. *Community Power Structure: A Study of Decision Makers.* Garden City, New York: Doubleday and Company, Incorporated, 1963.

Javits, Jacob. *Discrimination—USA.* New York: Harcourt, Brace and Company, 1960.

King, C. Wendell. *Social Movements in the United States.* New York: Random House, 1964.

King, Martin Luther, Jr. *Strength to Love.* New York: Pocket Books, Incorporated, 1964.

————. *Why We Can't Wait.* New York: Harper and Row, Incorporated, 1963.

Laidler, Harry W. *Social-Economic Movements.* New York: Thomas Y. Crowell Company, 1946.

Lewis, Anthony, and *The New York Times. Portrait of a Decade: The Second American Revolution.* New York: Random House, 1964.

Lincoln, C. Eric. *The Black Muslims in America*. Boston: Beacon Press, 1963.

Linton, Ralph (editor). *Acculturation in Seven American Indian Tribes*. New York: D Appleton-Century Company, Incorporated, 1940.

Lipset, S.M. *Agrarian Socialism: The Cooperative Commonwealth Federation in Saskatchewan*. Berkeley and Los Angeles: University of California Press, 1950.

Lockhart, William B., Yale Kamisar, and Jesse H. Choper. *Cases and Materials on Constitutional Rights and Liberties*. St. Paul: West Publishing Company, 1964.

Lomax, Louis E. *The Negro Revolt*. New York: The New American Library of World Literature, Incorporated, 1963.

Lubell, Samuel. *The Future of American Politics*. Garden City, New York: Doubleday and Company, Incorporated, 1956.

Macridis, Roy C. *The Study of Comparative Government*. PS 21 of *Studies in Political Science*. New York: Random House, 1964.

Mason, Alpheus T., and Richard H. Leach. *In Quest of Freedom*. Englewood Cliffs, New Jersey: Prentice-Hall, Incorporated, 1960.

McGill, Ralph. "The Meaning of Lincoln Today," in *American Issues: A Sourcebook For Speech Topics*. Edited by Edwin Black and Harry P. Kerr. New York: Harcourt, Brace and World, Incorporated, 1961.

Morton, Robert K. *Social Theory and Social Structure*. Glencoe, Illinois: The Free Press, 1957.

Michels, Robert. *Political Parties: A Sociological Study of the Oligarchical Tendencies Of Modern Democracy*. Translated by Eden and Cedar Paul. New York: Collier Books, 1962.

Myers, Henry Alonzo. *Are Men Equal? An Inquiry into the Meaning of American Democracy*. Ithaca, New York: Cornell University Press, 1955.

Neuman, Sigmund. *Permanent Revolution.* New York: Harper and Brothers, 1942.

Oppenheimer, Martin, and George Lakey. *A Manual for Direct Action.* Chicago: Quadrangle Books, Incorporated, 1964.

Peck, James. *Freedom Ride.* New York: Grove Press, Incorporated, 1962.

Peltason, Jack W. *Fifty-Eight Lonely Men.* New York: Harcourt, Brace and World, Incorporated, 1961.

Rodee, Carlton Clymer, Totton James Anderson, and Carol Quimby Christol. *Introduction to Political Science.* New York: McGraw-Hill Book Company, Incorporated, 1957.

Rogers, Williams P. *The Right to Vote,* in *American Issues: A Sourcebook for Speech Topics.* Edited by Edwin Black and Harry P. Kerr. New York: Harcourt, Brace and World Incorporated, 1961.

Rose, Arnold. *The Negro in America: The Condensed Version of Gunnar Myrdal's An American Dilemma.* New York: Harper and Row, 1964.

Selltiz, Claire, et al. *Research Methods in Social Relations.* New York: Holt, Rinehart and Winston, 1964.

Selznick, Philip. *The Organizational Weapon: A Study of Bolshevik Strategy and Tactics.* New York: McGraw-Hill Book Company, 1952.

Shridharanai, Krishnalal. *War Without Violence.* New York: Harcourt, Brace and Company, 1939.

Steinbeck, John. *Atque Vale,* in *American Issues: A Sourcebook for Speech Topics.* Edited by Edwin Black and Harry P. Kerr. New York: Harcourt, Brace and World, Incorporated, 1961.

Thompson, Daniel C. *The Negro Leadership Class.* Englewood Cliffs, New Jersey: Prentice-Hall, Incorporated, 1963.

Virginia Commission of Constitutional Government. *Did the Court Interpret or Amend?* Richmond: Virginia Commission on Constitutional Government, 1960.

Waring, Thomas R. *The Southern Case for Segregation*, in *American Issues: A Sourcebook for Speech Topics*. Edited by Edwin Black and Harry P. Kerr. New York: Harcourt, Brace and World, Incorporated, 1961.

White, Theodore H. *The Making of the President 1960*. New York: Pocket Books, Incorporated, 1962.

Wilson, James Q. *Negro Politics: The Search for Leadership*. Glencoe, Illinois: The Free Press, 1960.

Young, Whitney M., Jr. *To Be Equal*. New York: McGraw-Hill Book Company, 1964.

Zinn, Howard. *A Fate Worse Than Integration*, in *American Issues: A Sourcebook for Speech Topics*. Edited by Edwin Black and Harry P. Kerr. New York: Harcourt, Brace and World, Incorporated, 1961.

_____. *SNCC: The New Abolitionists*. Boston: Beacon Press, 1964.

Periodicals

After the Blood Bath, Newsweek, LXVI (August 30, 1965), 13-19.

Alabama: The Trial, Time, LXXXV (May 14, 1965), 27-29.

Alinsky, Saul. *A Professional Radical Moves in on Rochester: Conversations with Saul Alinsky, Part II, Harper's*, CCXXXI (July, 1965), 52-59.

_____. *The Professional Radical: Conversations with Saul Alinsky, Harper's*

CCXXX (June, 1965), 37-47.

Allport, Gordon W. (special editor). *Controlling Group Prejudice, The Annals Of the American Academy of Political and Social Science*, CCXLIV (March, 1946), 1-182.

Armstrong, Richard. *Will Snick Overcome? Post*, August 28, 1965, pp. 79-83.

Beach, Paul Cole, Jr. *The Politics of Race, The Intercollegiate Review*, I (February-March, 1965),72-74.

Becker, Howard S., and Blanche Geer. *Participant Observation and Interviewing: A Comparison, Human Organization,* XVI (Fall, 1957), 28-32.

"Bullets in Bogalusa," *Newsweek,* LXVI (July 19, 1965), 25-26.

"Civil Rights: Difference of Impact," *Time,* LXXXV (February 19,1965), 23.

"Civil Rights: Odd Cop Out," *Newsweek,* LXV (June 21, 1965), 30.

"Civil Rights: One War at a Time," *Newsweek,* LXVI (July 19, 1965), 22, 25.

"Civil Rights: The Central Point," *Time,* LXXXV (March 19,1965), 23-28.

"Civil Rights: The Deacons," *Newsweek,* LXVI (August 2, 1965), 28-29.

"Civil Rights: Trigger of Hope," *Time,* LXXXVI (August 20,1965), 19-20.

"Climax Near in Negro Revolt," *U.S. News and World Report,* LVIII (March 29, 1965), 27-29.

Cox, Oliver C. *Race Prejudice and Intolerance—A Distinction, Social Forces,* XXIV (December, 1945), 216-219.

Drinan, Robert F. *Why Direct Action Must Not Cease, Negro Digest,* XIV (April, 1965), 4-13.

Gross, Leonard. *America's Mood Today, Look,* XXIX (June 29, 1965), 15-21.

Heberle, Rudolf. *Observations on the Sociology of Social Movements, American Sociological Review,* XIV (June, 1949), 346-357.

Heinz, W.C., and Bard Lindeman. *The Meaning of the Selma March: Great Day at Trickem Fork, Post,* May 22, 1965, pp. 30-31, 89-95.

Hoffer, Eric. *A Time of Juveniles, Harper's,* CCXXX (June, 1965), 16-24.

Kendall, Willmoore. *The Civil Rights Movement and the Coming Constitutional Crisis, The Intercollegiate Review,* I (February-March, 1965), 53-71.

Laue, James H. *The Changing Character of Negro Protest, The Annals of the American Academy of Political and Social Science,* CCCLVII (January, 1965), 119-126.

Martin, Hosea L. *Negro Apathy: How to Combat It, Negro Digest,* XIV (March, 1965), 22-25.

Marx's Revenge, Time, LXXXV (May 21, 1965), 69.

May, John D. *Democracy, Organization, Michels, The American Political Science Review,* LIX (June, 1965), 417-429.

Mayer, Martin. *CORE: The Shock Troops of the Negro Revolt, Post,* November 21, 1964, pp.79-83.

McKenney, J. Wilson (editor). *Discrimination and Human Rights, CTA Journal,* LXI (March, 1965), 3-52.

Meir, August, Thomas S. Plaut, and Curtis Smothers. *Case Study in Nonviolent Direct Action, The Crisis,* LXXI (November, 1964), 573-578.

Melby, John F. *Racial Policy and International Relations, The Annals of the American Academy of Political and Social Science,* CCCIV (March, 1956), 132-136.

Morgan, Charles, Jr. *Southern Justice, Look,* XXIX (June 29, 1965), 72-73.

"New Crisis: The Negro Family," *Newsweek,* LXVI (August 9, 1965), 32-35.

"Organizations: Confusing the Cause," *Time,* LXXXVI (July 16, 1965), 20.

"Pinched Purses," *Time,* LXXXV (February 12, 1965), 17.

Playboy Interview: "Governor George Wallace, a Candid Conversation with Alabama's Demagogic Segregationist," *Playboy,* XI (November, 1964), 61-158.

Playboy Interview: "Martin Luther King, a Candid Conversation with the Nobel Prize-Winning Leader of the Civil Rights Movement," *Playboy,* XII (January, 1965), 65-78.

"Races: Confused Crusade," *Time,* LXXIX (January 12, 1962), 15.

"Races: Death and Transfiguration," *Time,* LXXXV (March 5, 1965), 23-25.

"Races: Trigger of Hate," *Time*, LXXXVI (August 20, 1965), 13-19.

Reddick, L.D. *What the Northern Negro Thinks About Democracy, The Journal of Educational Sociology*, XVII (January, 1944), 296-306.

Reid, Ira De A. (special editor). *Racial Desegregation and Integration, The Annals of The American Academy of Political and Social Science*, CCCIV (March, 1956), 1-143.

Rich, Marvin. *The Congress of Racial Equality and Its Strategy, The Annals of the American Academy of Political and Social Science*, CCCLVII (January, 1965), 113-118.

Rose, Arnold (special editor). *The Negro Protest, The Annals of the American Academy of Political and Social Science*, CCCLVII (January, 1965), 1-126.

Rustin, Bayard. *From Protest to Politics: The Future of the Civil Rights Movement, Commentary*, XXXIX (February, 1965), 25-31.

Steamer, R.J. *The Role of the Federal District Courts in the Segregation of Controversy, Journal of Politics*, XXII (August, 1960), 417-438.

Strong, Samuel M. *Negro-White Relations as Reflected in Social Types, The American Journal of Sociology*, LII (July, 1946), 23-30.

"The Man to Call When You Go to Jail," *Sepia*, XIII (January, 1964), 44-49.

"The South at War," *Ramparts*, IV (June, 1965), 17-52.

"The Unfinished Business of Negro Jobs," *Business Week*, June 12, 1965, pp. 82-106.

"The Various Shady Lives of the Ku Klux Klan," *Time*, LXXXV (April 9, 1965), 24-25.

Time Essay: "The Negro After Watts," *Time*, LXXXVI (August 27, 1965), 16-17.

Time Essay: "The Other South," *Time*, LXXXV (May 7, 1965), 48-49.

"Tough Years Ahead," *Newsweek*, LXVI (August 30, 1965), 19-20.

Trow, Margin.   Comment on *Participant Observing and Interviewing: A Comparison, Human Organization*, XVI (Fall, 1957), 33-35.

Warren, Robert Penn. *The Negro Now, Look*, XXIX (March 23, 1965), 23-31.

"What Southern Editors Say about the Negro Vote," *U.S. News and World Report*, LVIII (March 29, 1965), 34-38.

"What the Negro Vote Will Do to South," *U.S. News and World Report*, LVIII (March 29, 1965),30-34.

Wilkins, Roy. *The Challenge of Civil Rights, Washington University Magazine*, XXXV (Winter, 1965), 16-20.

Pamphlets

CORE.   *All About CORE*. New York: CORE, n.d.

_____. *Calendar of Coercion*. New York: CORE, 1964.

_____. *CORE Rules for Action*. New York: CORE, 1963.

_____.   *Instructions to Participants in Action Project*. Los Angeles: CORE, n.d.

_____. *Our Proposal to Make a Dream Come True*. Los Angeles: CORE, 1964.

_____. *Sales Bulletin on Buttons, Pins, and Stickers*. New York: CORE, n.d.

_____. *Sit Ins: The Student Report*. New York: CORE, May, 1960.

_____. *This is CORE*. New York: CORE, n.d.

_____. *Where is Democracy?* New York: Core, n.d.

NAACP. *NAACP: An American Organization*. New York: NAACP, 1964.

_____. *This is the NAACP*. New York: NAACP, 1964.

Ovington, Mary White. *How the National Association for the Advancement of Colored People Began.* New York: NAACP, originally printed in 1941.

SNCC. *Mississippi Freedom Project.* Atlanta: SNCC, n.d.

_____. *Mississippi Summer Project.* Atlanta: SNCC, 1964.

_____. *SNCC.* Atlanta: SNCC, 1963.

The Los Angeles Urban League. *Colleague.* Volume 10. Los Angeles: The Urban League, April, 1964.

UCRC. *UCRC Focus.* Los Angeles: UCRC, May, 1965.

Unpublished Material

CORE. *Constitution of the Los Angeles Congress of Racial Equality.* Los Angeles: CORE, 1963. (Mimeographed.)

Kuroda, Yusumasa. *A Cross-Cultural Analysis of the Desire for Political Power: Empirical Findings and Theoretical Implications.* Los Angeles: Research and Publication Fund, University of Southern California, 1964. (Mimeographed.)

_____, and Duane W. Hill. *Political Vocabulary.* Los Angeles: University of Southern California, Department of Political Science, 1964. (Mimeographed.)

Non-Violent Action Committee. *Short History of NVAC.* Los Angeles: NVAC, 1963. (Mimeographed.)

Newspapers

Ames, Walter, and Richard Main. "Right Protest Causes Federal Building Melee," *The Los Angeles Times*, March 10, 1965, pp.3, 27.

_____. "98 Arrested in Rights Melee Here," *The Los Angeles Times*, March 11, 1965, pp. 1,3.

Averill, John H. "CORE Leader Supports 1-Man, 1-Vote Ruling," *The Los Angeles Times*, June 26, 1965, p. 9.

_____. "Voting Rights Bill Signed at Historic Capitol Rite: Move to Implement Law

Begins," *The Los Angeles Times,* August 7, 1965, pp. 1, 14.

Bartlett, Charles. "Most Southern Republicans Are Aware of Need to Woo Negro Vote," *The Los Angeles Times*, March 11, 1965, p.5.

Beck, Paul. "Attempt to Move 1966 Convention from L.A. Discloses NAACP Rift," *The Los Angeles Times*, July 1, 1965, pp. 1, 16.

_____. "More Political Activity by Negroes Expected," *The Los Angeles Times*, June 30, 1965, p. 7.

_____. "NAACP Leaders Report Negro Big City Gains," *The Los Angeles Times*, July 5, 1965, pp. 2, 3.

Bernstein, Harry. "Automation Poses Negro Job Threat," *The Los Angeles Times*, July 5, 1965, pp. 1, 8.

_____. "Prejudice Remains, But Negroes Make Notable Gains on Labor Front," *The Los Angeles Times*, July 4, 1965, pp. 1, 3.

Blundell, William E. "A Shift in Strategy: Mass Demonstrations Begin to Lose Favor with Integration Forces," *The Wall Street Journal* (Pacific Coast Edition), August 27, 1963, pp. 1, 8.

Carlson, Elliot. "Integration at Work: Craft Unions' Barriers Against Negroes Begin to Fall in Many Cities," *The Wall Street Journal* (Pacific Coast Edition), May 18, 1965, pp. 1, 18.

Carson, Clay. "Faces of Protest: Woody Coleman," *Los Angeles Sentinel*, June 18, 1965, p. 4.

"Census Figures Reflect Negro Economic Level," *The Los Angeles Times*, May 8, 1965, p. 12.

Coles, Robert. "Family Life of the Negroes: The Cart---or the Horse?" *The Los Angeles Times*, October 17, 1965, p. 2.

Cordtz, Dan. "The Negro Vote: Widespread Antipathy to Goldwater May Tip Some States to LBJ," *The Wall Street Journal* (Pacific Coast Edition), October 9, 1964, pp.1, 18.

"Excerpts from Addresses at Lincoln Memorial during Capital Civil Rights March: Martin Luther King, Jr.," *The New York Times*, August 29, 1963, p.18.

Foley, Thomas J. "Discrimination Costs Placed at $23 Billion," *The Los Angeles Times*, March 26, 1965, p.23.

Gordon, Mitchell. "Race and Politics: Negroes Show Greater Local Political Power in Some Northern Cities," *The Wall Street Journal* (Pacific Coast Edition), April 9, 1964, pp. 1, 18.

Hebers, John. "Civil Rights: South Slowly Yields," *The New York Times*, December 20, 1964, p. E3.

Hoffer, Eric. "The Negro Is Prejudiced Against Himself," *The New York Times Magazine*, November 29, 1964, pp. 27-114.

Irwin, Don. "Mounted Police Route 600 in Montgomery," *The Los Angeles Times*, March 17, 1965, pp. 1, 2.

Jackson, Robert. "All Night Prayer Vigil Defies 8 L.A. Judges," *The Los Angeles Times*, March 13, 1965, p. 12.

Landauer, Jerry. "Indiana Backlash: Many Gary Democrats Who Supported Wallace To Vote for Goldwater," *The Wall Street Journal* (Pacific Coast Edition), July 30, 1964, pp. 1, 11.

Lewis, Anthony. "Civil Rights: Decade of Progress," *The New York Times*, December 20, 1964, p. E 3.

Maxwell, Neil. "Negro Campuses: Colleges in South Seek to Improve Facilities, Lift Academic Levels," *The Wall Street Journal* (Pacific Coast Edition), May 6 ,1964, pp.1, 9.

May, Roger B. "Integrating Suburbs: "Fair Housing" Groups Breach Racial Barriers in More Communities," *The Wall Street Journal* (Pacific Coast Edition), October 8, 1964, pp. 1, 14.

Negro 'Deacons' Claim They Have Machine Guns, Grenades for 'War," *The Los Angeles Times*, June 13, 1965, pp. 1, 16.

"Negro Judge Criticizes 16 CORE Members," *The Los Angeles Times*, December 1, 1964, p. 24.

"Negro Pastor Assails CORE Use of Children," *The Los Angeles Times*, April 26, 1965, p. 6.

Nelson, Jack.   "ACLU Attack Southern Justice," *The Los Angeles Times*, November 1, 1965, p.11.

_____.   "Arming of Negroes in Rights Fight Assailed," *The Los Angeles Times*, June 15,1965, p. 5.

_____.   "CORE Chief Urges New Negro Political Party," *The Los Angeles Times*, July 2, 1965, pp 1, 7.

_____.   "Dixie Political Revolt Begins," *The Los Angeles Times*, August 8, 1965, pp. 1, 2.

_____.   "Jim Crow Justice: Last Stronghold of Segregation," *The Los Angeles Times*, June 13, 1965, pp.1, 18.

_____.   "Justice Department Shirks: Alabama Court Charade Cries Out for Intervention," *The Los Angeles Times*, October 3, 1965, p. 2.

_____.   "King Sees Gain But Long Road," *The Los Angeles Times*, February 21, 1965, pp. 1, 2.

Pearson, Drew, "Here's an Up-to-Date Rundown of Klans Currently Operating," *The Los Angeles Times*, October 20, 1965, p. 6

_____.   "Negroes Arming 'to Fight Back,' Mississippi NAACP Head Says," *The Los Angeles Times*, September 1, 1965, p. 6.

"Riot at a Glance," *The Los Angeles Times*, August 16, 1965, p.1.

Stennis, John,   "Voting Rights Bill: 'Mockery of Constitution,'" *The Los Angeles Times*, March 28, 1965, pp 1, 2.

Tanner, James C. "Civil Rights Test: Negroes in South Ready Immediate Broad Drive to Try Out New Law," *The Wall Street Journal* (Pacific Coast Edition), July 1, 1964, pp. 1, 12.

_____.   "New Race Troubles: Negroes Ready Another Wave of Demonstrations Against Bias in South," *The Wall Street Journal* (Pacific Coast Edition), February 5, 1964, pp. 1, 13.

_____. "Southern Schools: Integration Spreads But Many Districts Find Ways to Thwart It," *The Wall Street Journal* (Pacific Coast Edition), September 2, 1964, pp. 1, 12.

Thompson, Robert E. "Race Problem Pointed Up in Moynihan Report," *The Los Angeles Times*, September 29, 1965, p. 4.

"Times Editorials: 'Civil Disobedience' and the Law," *The Los Angeles Times*, September 12, 1965, p.6.

"Times Editorials: Civil Rights and Wrong Protests," *The Los Angeles Times*, March 12, 1965, p.4.

"Times Editorials: Excesses in the Rights Movement," *The Los Angeles Times*, July 6, 1965, p. 4.

"Urban League to Aid Skilled Minority Groups," *The Los Angeles Times*, March 17, 1965, p. 2.

Weeks, Paul. "Break Hinted in Poverty Dilemma: CORE Holds Yorty Office Sit-In," *The Los Angeles Times,* May 29, 1965, p. 13.

_____. "CORE Defends Tactics at Legislative Hearing," *The Los Angeles Times,* December 4, 1964, p. 8.

_____. "Melee Hurts Negro Cause," *The Los Angeles Times,* March 11, 1965, p.3.

_____. "Solution to Problems in South L.A. Sought: Negroes Launch Their Own Operation 'Bootstrap,'" *The Los Angeles Times,* October 1, 1965, pp.1, 8.

_____. "Tactics Used Here Dismay Rights Leaders," *The Los Angeles Times,* March 12, 1965, pp. 3, 35.

Wilkins, Roy, "New Civil Rights Act Cannot Help But Affect Negro Groups' Tactics," *The Los Angeles Times,* November 30, 1964, p.5.

_____. "Rights Cause Demands Full-Time Application," *The Los Angeles Times,* July 19, 1965, p. 5.

"Wilkins Sees Good, Bad in Wake of L.A. Rioting," *The Los Angeles Times*, October 27, 1965, p.3.

Zimmerman, Fred L. "Changing Clinton," *The Wall Street Journal* (Pacific Coast Edition), August 27, 1965, p. 8.

_____. "Race and Violence: More Dixie Negroes Buy Arms to Retaliate Against White Attacks," *The Wall Street Journal,* (Pacific Coast Edition), July 12, 1965, pp. 1, 15.

Legal Citations

Brown v. Board of Education of Topeka, 347 U.S. 483; 74 S. Ct. 686; 98 L. Ed. 873 (1954).

Guinn v. United States, 238 U.S. 347; 35 S Ct, 926; 59 L. Ed. 1340 (1915).

Interviews

Hall, Robert, Co-Chairman of NVAC. Personal interview at NVAC office, Los Angeles, California, June 23, 1965.

Smith, Don. Chairman of CORE. Personal interview at CORE office, Los Angeles, California, June 23, 1965.

LaVergne, TN USA
03 February 2010
171920LV00005B/3/P